Monica

Monica

Christine Sutherland

CANONGATE

First published in Great Britain in 1991
by Canongate Press Plc,
14 Frederick Street, Edinburgh, Scotland.
First published in the United States of America
in 1990 by Farrar, Straus & Giroux

British Library Cataloguing in Publication Data
Sutherland, Christine
Monica: heroine of the Danish resistance
I. Title
940.53489092

ISBN 0 86241 337 0

Printed and bound in Great Britain by
Butler & Tanner Ltd, Frome, Somerset

Contents

List of Illustrations

On the wall of a thirteenth-century church on the island of Lolland in Denmark is a stone tablet commemorating Monica de Wichfeld, a local woman and a national heroine, condemned to death by the Germans shortly before the end of the Second World War. Lolland is an inclement and remote part of the world, but on most days fresh flowers somehow find their way to the tablet.

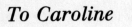

To Caroline

Monica

Prologue

IT IS MAY 13, 1944, in the fifth year of World War II. In England a powerful armada of over a million men is preparing to launch an assault on Fortress Europe. Fifteen hundred miles away to the east, the victorious Russian armies are driving the Germans westward toward Poland. In the Pacific, Admiral Nimitz's forces are about to hit Saipan and the Marianas, gateway to the reconquest of the Philippines. Everywhere the tide is turning against the Axis powers and throughout Europe sabotage and resistance to the occupation forces are increasing. But the Germans are a long way from being beaten; they retaliate mercilessly against those who dare to oppose them.

A court-martial is in progress at Dagmar House, the Gestapo headquarters in Copenhagen, a modern building overlooking the medieval town square. The accused are all members of the Danish Resistance. Their crime: giving aid to the enemies of the Reich. The room, vast, light, and crowded, in happier days served as the boardroom of a Danish industrial company. German soldiers in combat gear, submachine guns at the ready, line the white-painted walls; the atmosphere is tense, for after two days of trial a verdict is about to be announced.

The eleven prisoners are led in, one by one, and shown to seats in two rows of chairs—four in front, seven in back. Only the four special prisoners are ordered to the front row, three young men and an attractive woman in her late forties. She has a calm patrician face, dark hair elegantly parted and shot with gray at the temples, large gray eyes, and beautiful, carefully manicured hands. She is dressed in an expensive-looking brown tweed country suit with a fine cashmere sweater, wool stockings, and highly polished brogues. She takes her place, surveys the display of military might around her, and smiles faintly. She turns her head slightly to cast an affectionate glance at a tall, nineteen-year-old prisoner sitting directly behind her. It is her son Viggo; he was arrested some weeks ago, but she hopes he will soon be released.

Everybody stands as three judges enter the room and take their places at a long table on a raised dais under a picture of Adolf Hitler. The judges are in black SS uniforms with gray SS skull insignia on their lapels. Behind them comes the counsel for the prosecution, young, well-fed, and rosy-faced, his expression incongruously fashioned into a stone mask. The sentences are read out starting from the left of the front row:

"Georg Brockhoff Quistgaard—condemned to death." The young Dane looks uncomprehendingly at the judge for a second, then slumps down rigidly in his chair.

"Arne Lützen-Hansen," a brilliant radio operator recently parachuted from England, "condemned to death."

"Carl Jorgen Larsen," a cashier from the Århus Privatbank, who heroically supplied ammunition to the saboteurs in Zeeland, "condemned to death."

The judge pauses for a moment and casts his glance around the room. He has come to the case of the *Third Reich vs. Monica Wichfeld*, a tricky one. "Monica Emily Wichfeld," he intones, "condemned to death." The audience gasps. This is the first time since the Middle Ages that a woman has been condemned to death in Denmark. How dare the Germans do it? How will the country react?

Monica betrays no emotion. Conscious of her son sitting behind her, she pulls out her enameled Tiffany compact so she can see his face in the mirror, smiles at him, and slowly powders her nose. In the deathly silence which follows she looks at the judges and asks, "Anything else, gentlemen?"

"Yes, you have permission to make an application for mercy, if you wish," says the counsel for the prosecution.

"Does that apply to my companions?"

"No."

"Then it is of no interest." She reaches behind and squeezes her son's hand.

The sentences continue. Imprisonment from two to twelve years for five prisoners and two acquittals, one of whom, on the grounds of his youth and insufficient evidence, is Viggo.

While she is being led back to her cell, Monica addresses one of her fellow prisoners, who seems to be plunged in deep gloom. "Cheer up," she says in her English-accented Danish, "this surely is a unique experience—you can only go through it once. We are lucky."

One

Ireland

MONICA MASSY-BERESFORD was born at her father's house, 7 Eaton Square, London, at the height of a raging summer storm on July 12, 1894. As the gilt clock on the tower of nearby St. Peter's Church, where her parents had been married the year before, struck the night hours, Monica arrived in an England at the apogee of Victorian splendor. The queen's Diamond Jubilee was three years away, but already George Massy-Beresford, Irish landowner and sportsman, was busy arranging for seats in the Abbey. He was also eager to return to County Fermanagh in northern Ireland in time for the sailing regattas on Lough Erne. He had grown impatient awaiting the baby's arrival, for Monica was a week late. Much to the annoyance of his wife, Alice, they set off when their daughter was barely ten days old.

The channel crossing to Ireland was so rough that Miss King, the recently engaged nurse, who had never traveled by sea and had no idea where Ireland was, begged them to "get off the boat and continue the journey by land." After the terrible crossing and a train ride, it was midnight by the time they arrived at the railroad station where they were to be met. But something had gone wrong with the telegraph system and their coachman was not there. How was the party to get to the ferry and cross Lough Erne? While Mrs. Beresford, with the baby and the now hysterical nanny, sat in the tiny waiting room, surrounded by mountains of luggage, her husband ransacked the village for some sort of conveyance. What he found was a hearse driven by six horses, with black and silver plumes in their manes, returning from a funeral and the aftermath of an Irish wake at the local pub.

"It was a pretty ancient vehicle," Monica's mother recalled in a memoir written for her grandchildren. "At one time it must have been a splendid coach, but by now, with its tattered lining, cracked windows, and overpowering smell of whiskey and stale tobacco, it left a lot to be desired. But at least it was big enough for all of us and our luggage and we were glad to be rescued." The ferryman and his wife had to be aroused from bed to row the family across Lough Erne. "It was 3 a.m. and pitch dark, with rain pelting down on our heads, as we scrambled from the landing up the path to our house," she continued. "The baby, who had been angelic until now, showed its disapproval by loud wails. Our house servants were naturally all asleep. When they heard us banging on the doors, they assumed the house was on fire and rushed out onto the lawn in their nightgowns shouting wildly. Calm was eventually restored, the baby's bottle was heated, she was bathed and finally put to bed. Monica's arrival in Ireland was eventful, as her life was to be."

St. Hubert's was a comfortable Victorian house, acquired by the Dean of Kilmore, Monica's grandfather, for his wife, whose family owned nearby Crom Castle, vast, sprawling, and turreted, which stood on a bluff overlooking a majestic sweep of upper Lough Erne. "Our life in those peaceful pre-1914 days was ideal," Monica's mother remembered. And so indeed it was for most of the Anglo-Irish families, the so-called Protestant Ascendancy, scattered throughout the island in castles, Anglican rectories, pleasant country houses, and Georgian terraces. Most of them had lived in Ireland for centuries and thought of themselves as Irish, but their allegiance to the crown of England was absolute.

The Massy-Beresford family came from Irish-Scottish stock. The two names were combined in the middle of the nineteenth century when the Reverend Dean Massy, Monica's grandfather, married Sarah Beresford, heiress of Captain George Beresford, a Scottish landowner who had died of wounds in the Crimean War. As the Reverend John Massy was Dean of Kilmore and vicar of three parishes in Fermanagh, he was bound by his duties to spend a large amount of time in his Irish diocese. This pleased his wife, who loved the country around Lough Erne and enjoyed the company of her cousins, whose houses were scattered around the lake.

George Massy-Beresford, Monica's father, grew up with considerable expectations, as sole heir to the family's Scottish estates and to his father's place at St. Hubert's. He led a carefree life of hunting, shooting, and fishing, but one of his main passions was sailing on Lough Erne. His friends despaired of his ever getting married. He appeared to be a confirmed bachelor-sportsman, but one day when he was already past thirty-six, while attending a cricket match at Ballywalter Park, Lord Dunleath's Italianate country house near Belfast, he met and fell in love with the owner's daughter Alice, more than thirteen years his junior. He married her and they went to live at St. Hubert's. It was said locally that Alice's main attraction for him was her money, for by then George's extravagant life-style had dispersed much of the Massy-Beresford inheritance. Alice's father, John Mulholland, who became Lord Dunleath, was Ireland's second-richest man, with a fortune based on the manufacture of textiles. He was one of the tycoons of the province who rose to power and wealth during the industrial revolution, and Alice was his youngest daughter.

The newly married couple embodied different attitudes to life and were temperamentally unsuited. The delicate, romantic, highly strung, exquisitely educated girl, conversant in French and German, whose favorite place in the world was her father's house on the French Riviera at Cannes, soon discovered that she had little in common with the high-living, heavy-drinking, authoritarian athlete whose life was totally dedicated to sport. But like many a Victorian wife before her, Alice found consolation in her children. After Monica two sons—Tristram and John Clarina—were born in quick succession, followed some six years later by Desmond, whose arrival was greeted with surprise and annoyance by his siblings.

Monica's memories of her childhood were centered on St. Hubert's and the lake. Comfortable and thoroughly lived in, with deep windowsills, faded chintz, and a profusion of flowers, food, and servants, the house was surrounded by gardens and an extensive parkland, with the lawns sweeping down to a lake that was always alive with white sails. Lough Erne played a vital part in the lives of the Massy-Beresford family and their neighbors. It had to be crisscrossed constantly to get back to what was known as "civilization" in the shape of the nearest town, with its grocer, doctor, dentist, and railway station. One went to church on Sunday in a motorboat, one was christened or buried on the other side of the lough in Enniskillen, with the coffin transported across the lake on a flat barge.

The children remembered their home, St. Hubert's, as beautiful. "Enormous flowering rhododendrons and miles and miles of gorse that smelled like butter," Monica's brother Tim (Tristram) recalled. "We romped through it with our dogs, waded in the streams, which to us children were rivers flowing to mysterious pirate-infested seas; we sailed our little toy boats in peaty pools among the rocks on the shore, played hide-and-seek in the garden or crept about in the twilight looking for fairies. There was magic at St. Hubert's. I can't imagine why we chose to grow up."

With all its attractions, St. Hubert's was a remote paradise. Eight miles of hilly, pot-holed, gravelly road separated it from Belturbet, the nearest station on the antiquated single-track railway. The only place that could have been called a town in those days was Enniskillen, twenty miles in the opposite direction and easier to reach by boat. "There were few neighbors with children approaching our age," Monica's brother remembered, "so we were pretty much thrown onto our own devices."

"Monica was the undisputed leader of our group," wrote Brigadier Tim Massy-Beresford in a short memoir of their childhood. "She had all the ideas and saw to it that we carried them out. More often than not, these were things strictly forbidden, often dangerous, like bathing on some remote rocky shore, or sailing a boat long before we were allowed to handle one, or jumping from a particularly high trampoline in the barn. . . . She knew no fear and egged her brothers on. From an early age she had a clear-cut personality and a will she could impose not only on her brothers but on children who happened to be around or came to visit."

The dark-haired, gray-eyed tomboy was much loved by the country people on the lake. It would not have been surprising for a child brought up in such circumstances to have had an exaggerated idea of her own self-importance, yet Monica had none. She was always completely natural with everyone around her. A local farmer was asked by his wife what made him admire Miss Monica so much. "Is it the beauty of her?" "No, it's not that," he answered, "it's her freedom."

Reserved by nature and essentially a loner, she seldom shared her thoughts with anyone except her younger brother Jack (John Clarina). Three years younger than Monica, fair and slender, blessed with a cheerful disposition and wonderful Irish wit, Jack was physically fearless and as independent as his formidable sister. Unlike their amiable brother Tim, Jack did not hesitate to stand up to Monica. "Why won't you do this for me?" she would wail; "Tim would have done it." "Well, you see, I am not Tim" came the answer, and she was left furious but filled with grudging respect. Though their wills clashed constantly, they remained the closest of friends, sharing a passion for books and spinning dreams.

Neither Monica nor Jack was particularly close to their parents when they were children. The dominating influence over Monica in her childhood was Miss Jell, a governess with an original mind who taught her how to think independently and encouraged the young girl's insatiable desire to learn about life beyond the shores of Lough Erne. It was to Miss Jell that Monica owed her wide knowledge of history, which in later years used to impress so many of the distinguished people she met in England, Italy, and Denmark. But much as she admired the remarkable Miss Jell, who remained in the family until her death twenty years later, the only person Monica would ever confide in was Jack. He was the one who shared her thoughts and her dreams. The relationship endured far beyond schoolroom, adolescence, and Monica's marriage. His death in the final months of World War I was a blow from which she never recovered.

There were fewer than a dozen homes on Lough Erne. Although they were only miles apart, traveling from one to another was complicated and time-consuming along the indented lakeshore. Everything centered on the lake. The resident families and their guests existed for yacht racing, fishing, rowing, or driving about in steam launches or motorboats. The highlight of the summer was the annual regatta at Crom Castle. "Dozens of white sails drifting past the winning post in the gold-amber light of a calm September evening; animated (sometimes acrimonious) discussions in the boathouse; and Lady Erne in a green-and-white sweeping tea gown pouring out tea for hungry crews until her wrist ached," recalled Alice Massy-Beresford in her memoir. It was a peaceful existence in a world of blue distances, where pollution was unknown, where the clouds driven from the Mountains of Mourne brought rain that was gentle and pure. Days were passed in country pursuits that followed the unchanging cycle of the seasons and the flow of the currents in the lake.

There were journeys to the English countryside—cumbersome tribal affairs, with endless trunks, dogs, etc.—where George Massy-Beresford hunted for a few months every winter. There were also brief stays in London, with assorted cousins and friends; then back home to beloved St. Hubert's and the lake.

For a few weeks each summer they took a cottage in Bundoran on the Donegal coast, a primitive spot of wild beauty, where the western sea hurled itself against rocks and the tides were treacherous. But there were large warm pools among the rocks where the children could learn how to swim, with bushes of wild raspberries and tamarisk concealing them. There was shrimping on the long summer evenings, and fishing for mackerel by moonlight. "There was laughter and youth at Bundoran," Monica recalled years later. "We walked as far as we dared on the rocks up the long, narrow path to the moon, singing, drifted to bed, and went to sleep lulled by the beat and suck of the tide and the gulls overhead fussing."

One lake family that the Massy-Beresford children particularly enjoyed visiting were the Brookes of Colebrook. Sheila Brooke was Monica's contemporary and her brothers were Tim's and Jack's ages; she later married Harry Mulholland, Monica's cousin. Colebrook, a fine Georgian house, was only fifteen miles away as the crow flies, but getting there was a day's journey for the children. "One had to row across the lake, bicycle or ride five miles to the local railway station, change trains after two stops, and then bicycle again to Colebrook House," recalled Tim Beresford. "But we loved going there; we often spent a week at a time, and these visits were landmarks for us with their gaiety and fun."

In keeping with established tradition, Monica's brothers were sent to boarding school in England long before they even entered their teens, while Mrs. Massy-Beresford arranged for Sheila Brooke to come to St. Hubert's to keep Monica company during her lessons. It was an inspired move, for left alone, the thirteen-year-old Monica wandered about disconsolate and rebellious, more and more at war with her father. Photographs of the period show a determined heart-shaped face hiding under a mop of dark hair, looking somewhat discontented. Monica greeted Sheila's arrival with joy; it was the beginning of a friendship which lasted until death.

After an attempt to send Monica to boarding school at

fifteen had misfired (she was sacked for nonconformist behavior after a month), her mother sent her and Sheila Brooke
to spend a few months with a family in Tours to learn French.
Next came a finishing school in Paris, where Monica distinguished herself by winning a history prize for an essay on
"The Era of Napoleon." She had developed a tremendous
interest in the French emperor and insisted on visiting various
sites connected with his life. Sheila Brooke recalls accom-
panying her to Les Invalides one holiday and being "desperately drenched while waiting in line to get in." The next
stop in the girls' education was Dresden.

One October morning in 1910 Alice Massy-Beresford, a
fair, delicate Englishwoman in her late thirties, accompanied
by two teenage girls and a mountain of luggage, stepped off
the night express from Cologne and drove to the house of
Fräulein Höricks on a leafy street near the river Elbe. Under
Fräulein Höricks's tutelage the girls, both sixteen, were to be
initiated into the mysteries of the German language, German
history, and the Dresden art treasures.

Dresden, the old capital of the Saxon kings, was one of
the most stimulating towns in the German-speaking world,
second only to Vienna. It sparkled with life and reverberated
with music. When Richard Strauss's new opera *Salome* was
barred from performance in Berlin and Vienna on the grounds
of sacrilege, Ernst von Schuch, the conductor of the Dresden
Royal Opera, presented it on October 9, 1905. The audience
responded with enthusiasm, extending to thirty-eight curtain
calls for both the composer and the conductor. At the time of
the Massy-Beresford arrival, there was talk of *Der Rosenka-
valier* being performed, and its premiere took place on January 26, 1911.

Along Dresden's elegant leafy boulevards a cosmopolitan crowd shopped for exquisite china and visited silversmiths, jewelers, and glassmakers. Since the time of Augustus the Strong, who founded the nearby Meissen factory, it had been customary for the upper class and bourgeois families of Central Europe to order their wedding trousseaux in Dresden and to travel to Meissen to buy china. The city was an important trade center and a magnet for painters, writers, musicians, and artisans. Besides the famous royal palace and the opera house, it had a dozen theaters, ten concert halls, and numerous art galleries, of which the magnificent Central Art Gallery and the Zwinger were the most famous. To a sixteen-year-old girl, brought up in a remote Irish province, it became a joyous revelation, a world she had been longing for. "I prayed that one day I would leave this place and travel far," she told Jack while reminiscing about their childhood by the shores of Lough Erne.

Fräulein Höricks lived in a roomy, comfortable apartment on a fine street near the Elbe. Out of Monica's window could be seen the recently restored thirteenth-century Gothic Sophienkirche. Their week was punctuated by visits to museums, concert halls, picture galleries, and classes in drawing, fencing, and German. The girls found the language easy to master. Tuesday night was theater night, followed by a supper party attended by young people, mostly students from Dresden University. On Saturdays there was dancing, in which Monica excelled. It became apparent to everyone that the ten months she spent in Dresden transformed Monica physically from a lumpy tomboy teenager into a slender seventeen-year-old girl who moved and walked gracefully, spoke excellent German, and exuded self-confidence. Fräulein Höricks and the Dresden ambiance contributed a great deal, but the most dramatic change was attributed to her gifted dancing teacher, Herr Töplitz. Sheila Brooke recalled that Herr Töplitz "was amazed" by Monica's rare sense of rhythm and natural co-ordination. "She had perfect timing and could effortlessly master new steps, gliding over Herr Töplitz's parquet floors without missing a beat, light as a feather, her entire body fluid, like a ballerina's." After six months of Herr Töplitz's lessons, she was winning every competition at the school. "It is being suggested that I remain in Dresden and train to become a professional ballroom dancer," Monica happily related in one of her letters home. The very idea was enough to bring Mrs. Massy-Beresford hurrying back to Dresden. "It was about time," as Sheila Brooke rather primly recalled, "for Monica had by then acquired an entire host of male admirers, not all of whom would have won her mother's approval." Fräulein Höricks produced a never-ending succession of conventional, heel-clicking youths, scions of the Junker gentry, but much to her dismay Monica found them tedious and preferred the young painters and singers of Dresden's bohemia. The law-abiding Sheila Brooke rarely deviated from Fräulein Höricks's rules, but Monica as usual was keen to assert her independence.

"I remember Monica in those Dresden days," Sheila recorded in her reminiscences. "Was she beautiful? That's difficult to say; she was still a teenager. But her deep gray eyes, set wide apart, her dark eyebrows, that high forehead and wavy abundant hair were delightful; her figure was a little bit too athletic at first, though she danced beautifully. I remember the ballet master telling the class that Fräulein Monica could get an engagement with any dance company in Europe if she wanted." Sheila went on to describe Monica's interest in history and her love of languages. "Before her arrival in Dresden she could speak fluent French, and now she picked up German with the greatest of ease. She was original and vivacious and had an ability to establish instant, spontaneous rapport with the people around her. No wonder she became popular and that the young men flocked to her."

Monica was now seventeen; she had been in Dresden for over a year and it was time to go home. Her father was about to leave on a protracted trip to North America with his friend Lord Hugh Grosvenor "to look for gold," a venture that proved financially disastrous and ruinous to the health of both men. Alice Massy-Beresford wanted her only daughter back in England; reports from Dresden convinced her that Monica was perhaps growing up too fast for her own good.

The girls and Alice returned to England in late autumn and set off on a round of visits to Scotland. Staying at lovely Ballindalloch Castle with Sir John and Lady Macpherson, Monica held sway in the drawing room, conversing brilliantly about her cosmopolitan life in Dresden. "There were several girls in the house party, all of them very much older but listening to her opinions with respect," her mother noted with amusement. "They were quite disconcerted when they discovered that Monica was only seventeen. I was reading a book at the time, entitled *The Diary of an Old Soul.* I could not help thinking that my daughter was certainly an 'old soul.' Ever since she was a baby she had a kind of uncanny maturity about her; it tempered her wildness of spirit."

After a short stay in London to await her father's return from America, they returned to Ireland for Christmas. That winter Monica was allowed to attend a few dances in Dublin. She enjoyed the spectacle of candlelit Georgian ballrooms in some of the fine Dublin houses, but found the young men provincial, and clumsy dancers to boot. With most of her

contemporaries Dublin was only a dry run before entry into
the real world, the London season and presentation at
court, a ritual obligation in those days. This was duly performed the next May. White dress, long train, white feathers,
and elbow-length gloves were acquired. Accompanied by her
mother, Monica drove to Buckingham Palace to be presented
to George V and Queen Mary. It was noted by one of those
present that "the Queen gave Monica a friendly smile," and
that Monica accomplished the difficult task of retreating back-
ward gracefully, no mean feat, since her gown had the reg-
ulation nine-foot train.

London in the last summers before the outbreak of World
War I was gripped by an almost frenetic gaiety. The memoirs
of the period recall the splendor of the season, enhanced by
beautiful summer weather. In the squares of Mayfair and
Belgravia, at countless houses, Monica was received and entertained. She was popular as a fine dancer and an amusing
conversationalist, usually surrounded by good-looking men
living in a halcyon world soon to disintegrate.

Did she fall in love during the season? She was often
seen with one man, Dickie Ashley, a cousin of Edwina Mountbatten. He was different from the usual run of Guards officers,
sporty types Monica swore she would never marry. It is unlikely that she and Ashley discussed marriage before he was
killed in Flanders during the first year of the war. They were
still young and there seemed to be so much time for everything
in the privileged circle to which Monica belonged. On Friday
evenings during spring, summer, and autumn, the golden
young left London to congregate at a party in some country
house, where they played tennis and croquet. H. G. Wells's
game "Little Wars," based on his scientific anti-war ro-
mances, was now the rage, and summer afternoons were spent

on manicured lawns, moving toy soldiers about. It was only a game, but as the summer days shortened, a feeling spread that perhaps the game might become real.

They were back at St. Hubert's with a house party of friends, playing His Master's Voice records on the huge horned gramophone. The weather in Ireland that summer was unusually beautiful, but a jarring note was injected by Tim, Monica's brother, who announced that war with Germany was imminent. It would begin in late summer after the Kiel Canal was opened and the harvest was in. Tim had left Eton at Christmas and was now at Sandhurst, to be commissioned an officer that autumn. No one quite believed his predictions. Yet the local people reported that "strange, eerie things were beginning to happen on the lake." There had been talk of a little man, a leprechaun, who "walked across the water in the direction of Castle Crom." Almost a fixture of the place, he had been seen by the postman and the clergyman's daughter, Mrs. Ringwood, considered a reliable witness. But this time strange lights, "brighter than any electric lamp," lit up the lake after sunset and caused anxiety to spread. Lord Erne of Crom Castle, who "was much bothered by them," wrote a letter to the *Irish Times* asking if anyone could provide an explanation, but no satisfactory answer was forthcoming. When he consulted an old history of Lough Erne, he learned that the same phenomenon had occurred once before, in the summer before the "great troubles."

"All of a sudden there was presage of a catastrophe in the air," Mrs. Massy-Beresford noted in her diary. "I remember Monica saying to me on the evening after Tim had departed for Sandhurst, 'It feels strange—as if almost anything might happen!' "

Locally matters had been on the boil for two years. The Ulster loyalists, who comprised most of the Protestant families in Northern Ireland, were determined to remain part of England and were violently opposed to the Irish Home Rule Bill introduced by Prime Minister Asquith in 1912. Various illegal arms shipments were seized, and Alice Massy-Beresford's brother, Lord Dunleath, was threatened with arrest at one point. "The idea of arresting this most patriotic of men was outrageous and comic," his sister wrote in her diary. "Thank God we refused to be cast adrift from our mother country; we have to guard the back door to the kingdom in case of war." Monica was too young and too full of her own life to take politics seriously, but she wore orange-colored lilies on her dress to show that her sympathies lay with her family.

On June 28, 1914, Monica and her mother were motoring through the little town of Belturbet in her father's "one-mouse-power" Panchard, when they saw news placards announcing the murder of Archduke Franz Ferdinand at Sarajevo. "Little did we think what that meant, as our minds were full of our local troubles and preoccupied with a cousin's wedding at which Monica was to be one of the bridesmaids," recalled Alice Massy-Beresford. "And anyway, what could events in faraway Serbia have to do with us?" A little over five weeks later, war was declared. Tim came over from Sandhurst to say goodbye, before joining his regiment. "We forced ourselves to appear cheerful for his sake, but foreboding, like a sinister black bird, constantly hovered over our heads."

The next few months were terrible. Alone with her mother in the house, both of them avidly scanning the papers, Monica saw her friends reported wounded or killed, one by one. In late October, the mail brought a picture magazine with a row of photographs of young guardsmen recently killed in action in Flanders. Each man had been a friend or a partner at some recent dance. Monica put the paper down and cried. George Massy-Beresford, who at sixty was too old to enlist, decided to join the Ambulance Corps; he later spent two years in France as a driver.

In late autumn Monica and her mother traveled to England to pay family visits. On arriving at Liverpool Street Station from Norfolk, where they had been staying with friends, they saw the entire station full of stretchers—hundreds and hundreds of wounded coming home after the Battle of Ypres. In that battle Teddy Mulholland, Monica's first cousin, was killed. Already Henry Crichton, another cousin, and neighbors Hugh Grosvenor, Gerry Ward, and many others had been killed. Then came news of Lord Erne's death; his seven-year-old grandson inherited the title and Crom Castle. An epoch ended with Lord Erne's death. No more would the white sails drift past the winning post on September evenings, no more Christmas gatherings or servants' dances at Crom with Lady Erne and the butler leading "Sir Roger de Coverley," and no more evening carols at the church. The strange bright warning lights had truly prophesied the end of a happy era.

Monica left Ireland early in 1915. She obtained a job in a soldiers' canteen in the East End of London, where every day she served countless cups of tea to British Tommies and scrubbed yards and yards of floors.

Two

Jorgen

FAIR-HAIRED, of medium height, with fine regular features, Jorgen de Wichfeld belonged to a landowning family in southern Denmark. At age twenty-two, following the death of his father, Henning Wichfeld, chamberlain to Christian X and a prominent courtier, he inherited vast family estates— some three thousand acres of the richest farmland in Denmark. There were woods, a lakeshore, pedigreed livestock, and a family trust that had been set up in 1777. Educated in fashionable schools in Denmark and Switzerland, young Jorgen had never been taught how to manage an agricultural estate. Suddenly finding himself with a large disposable income, he decided to spend it seeing the world. Leaving his mother and his young sister Addi at Engestofte, the family seat, looked after by a houseful of servants, and the management of the farms in the hands of the local agent, Jorgen set off on his grand tour. During the next seven years, until the outbreak of World War I, he visited Egypt, Palestine, North Africa, England, France, Italy, and Germany. He also paid a long visit to Russia, staying with friends at the Danish legation in St. Petersburg. Maurice Baring, who happened to be there at the time, recalled young Wichfeld as a charming, though slightly effeminate young man, good at dancing and much in demand at court balls.

When his "devastatingly good-looking" younger brother Axel married Mabelle Moore, heiress to the Swift meat-packing fortune of Chicago, Jorgen embarked for New York, determined to see the New World in great style. Mabelle and Axel saw to it that he was included in their coast-to-coast travels, always in luxurious private Pullman trains with attendant butlers and maids. They introduced him to famous hostesses, so that soon after his arrival Jorgen became a fixture of Newport summers and Palm Beach winters. This agreeable life was suddenly interrupted by the outbreak of World War I, in which Denmark was to remain neutral. Jorgen returned to Europe, landing at Southampton. During a brief visit to Denmark, which after the excitement of the United States seemed to him more boring than ever, he decided to return to England and volunteered to join the staff of the Danish legation in London, where he was appointed honorary attaché. The legation was like a small family club: the ambassador was a friend of the Wichfelds, and other posts were filled by close friends and neighbors from Lolland. It was possible to travel between London and Denmark during the war. Jorgen paid occasional visits to his estate, riding and shooting with neighbors, but he always hurried back to wartime London after his dull stay in the country. Life in England was cheap for Danish nationals, and Jorgen, with an annual income of about $30,000, a huge amount of money in those days, led a very pleasant existence.

He maintained an opulent flat in Mayfair and was soon part of fashionable London, or whatever was left of it after the disasters of the German offensive on the Somme and the first Battle of Ypres. Though England was at war, London was still filled with pleasures. Jorgen was thirty, unattached, rich, and good-looking. With the prevailing shortage of men he was very much in demand. During the first year of the war he drifted into an unofficial engagement to a girl from the Netherlands, Alix van der Heit, who had come to England some years earlier in search of a husband. In the summer of 1915, while doing an occasional stint in a soldiers' canteen in Leicester Square, Alix met Monica Beresford and on the spur of the moment asked her to her engagement party later that week, a move she never ceased to regret. Describing her rich and well-connected fiancé, she showed Monica a picture of Engestofte, her future home.

"In the course of my life," Monica wrote many years later, "I have occasionally had moments of something close to extrasensory perception, as if in a flash a veil would suddenly lift uncovering my future. Such a moment occurred when Alix showed me the sepia photograph of Engestofte and the lake. I experienced a kind of instant recognition and *knew* this was going to be my home." This seemed absurd even to her, at the time. She thought no more about it and went off to the party at Oddenino's, chaperoned by her mother. Jorgen did not impress her much at that first meeting; he appeared pleasant, talked knowledgeably to her mother about pictures and Delft china, and seemed to be more of a success with the older generation than with her own. She noted that he was not very attentive to Alix, as one would have expected of a fiancé, but she put it down to his being foreign, an often-used explanation for odd behavior. She said she forgot about him the next day.

But it was quite different for Jorgen. Monica interested him from the start. The dark-haired Irish girl with gray-green eyes and a dazzlingly white complexion, who had such an original way of expressing herself and could transform a dull evening with her laughter and wit, appealed to his languid, conventional nature. She was like a magnet around whom people instinctively gathered. What a wonderful hostess she would make. In spite of his engagement to Alix, Jorgen was not seriously contemplating marriage at the moment. His experience with women was limited; his sexual drive had never been very strong. There had been moments in his life when he felt he could have turned away from marriage altogether. On the other hand, there was constant pressure from his mother to marry and produce an heir for Engestofte. For centuries the place had passed directly from father to son. It was inconceivable, he knew, for the chain of succession to be broken.

It was Monica's vivacity and scintillating conversation that appealed to Wichfeld above all. Looking at her, past her "dreadful clothes" and unflattering hairdo, he could see how she could be made to look elegant, even beautiful. She had wonderful hands, lovely shoulders and arms; he would take her to Paris and transform her. Next to Monica, Alix appeared mousy provincial. He decided to distance himself gently from his fiancée, which he hoped would result in her breaking off the engagement (which she did, marrying an admiral instead).

Much of the entertainment in wartime London consisted of impromptu gatherings of young people, arranged for the benefit of soldiers home on leave from the front. Accompanied by chaperones—mothers, aunts, and older sisters—girls like Monica dined at small restaurants in the city. They then went on to a friend's house and danced till midnight or later. "I noticed that a Mr. de Wichfeld, attaché at the Danish legation, turns up wherever we happen to be," wrote Mrs. Massy-

Beresford in a letter to her son Tim at the front. "He seems to be quite interested in Monica. I find him easy to talk to and very well educated; his clothes are elegant and he wears his monocle as if it were a part of himself; but of course he is a foreigner."

One evening Monica, together with several friends from the canteen where she worked, arranged a Dutch-treat party at the Café Royal in Regent Street. Most of the men were officers on leave from France, and as the evening progressed, more and more people joined in, among them Jorgen de Wichfeld. "I was just about to suggest we go home," recalled Monica's mother. "It was nearing midnight and the girls had an early start at the canteen the next morning, when the orchestra struck the opening bars of the 'Blue Danube.' Without formally asking her, Jorgen came up to Monica and led her onto the dance floor; they danced together in a way that I have never seen a couple dance before. And I was not the only one who thought so. Other couples soon left the floor to stare, for here were two people dancing to a Viennese waltz as Strauss would have wished to see it. Monica's dress stood out in a whirl around her, while the leader of the orchestra followed them across the floor with his violin, and played just for them."

Was it dancing that brought them together? It certainly made Monica pay more attention to her Danish admirer. But soon she began to discover various other points in his favor. His sophistication and gentle wit set him apart from the young men she had known up to then. With the exception of young Ashley, her male friends were hearty, unsophisticated countrymen dedicated to hunting, shooting, and fishing, very much in her father's mold. She did not know the worldly, scintillating group that formed around her contemporary Diana

Manners (later Lady Diana Cooper), an exclusive, slightly raffish coterie to which newcomers were rarely admitted. Monica would certainly have been able to hold her own among them, but London society, far more than that of any other European capital, was a series of close-knit, occasionally interlocking circles, very hard to break into. In all the wisdom of her twenty years, Monica was determined that her life be exciting. Of course there was a war going on, but it was bound to end. And then what? Was her fate to be married to a conventional country squire, perhaps in Ireland or Scotland, followed by years of frustration, like that of her mother? Not for her. The times in Dresden, Paris, and Tours had revealed an attractive life-style and a world to which Jorgen held the key. He was almost eleven years older and he was rich.

Among Monica's friends there was a kind of geronto-philic snobbery; older men were considered more attractive and entertaining, and better hosts than callow youths. Jorgen of course had a great advantage over his English rivals. Though he himself felt no shame at belonging to a neutral country and holding a diplomatic job while others fought, his was not an enviable position to be in. There were moments when he was conscious of unspoken hostility at his courting an English girl at a time when her countrymen on short leave from the front wanted her undivided attention. Yet he per-sisted in his pursuit.

Was Monica in love with this languid, monocled Dane? "She likes him, they seem to enjoy each other's company, but is she in love?" Mrs. Massy-Beresford wondered in one of her letters to Tim. Never having been truly in love, Monica had no answer to this question. She found Jorgen comfortable to be with; she admired his natural friendliness, his amusing and civilized conversation, and the elegance of his clothes. Her Victorian upbringing and her own inexperience precluded discussions about sex; had she thought more about it, she might have had some doubts on that score. At it was, she delayed her decision for a few months but finally gave way to Jorgen's urging. Their engagement was formally announced in *The Times*.

The family's reaction could hardly have been called enthusiastic. Her brother Tim, the army man, described it in one of his letters: " 'J,' as we all call him, has a good sense of humor and is very good-natured and generous, but quite futile and a trifle effeminate in his motions and way of speaking. He is utterly vague and woolly when anything serious is being discussed, but his saving grace is that he does not mind being teased unmercifully when he has made a particularly inane remark. His strong points are dancing and bridge, which initially must have attracted him to Monica. But what else?" Monica's father, who detested foreigners, was appalled. No use pointing out that Queen Alexandra herself was a Danish princess. The prospect of his only daughter disappearing into a foreign land was the last thing he wanted. Having met Jorgen only once, he pronounced him "too delicate to be able to shoot, ride, or sail"—a complete dismissal in his eyes. Monica's mother liked Jorgen and disagreed with Tim's scathing assessment of his future brother-in-law. "He knows a lot about china, furniture, and many nice things in this life," Alice reminded her critical son. But she too did not relish the prospect of Monica marrying a foreigner.

Objections to their marriage on the Danish side were based on historical grounds. Jorgen's mother, granddaughter of a Danish prime minister, had never forgotten (or forgiven after so many years!) Nelson's unprovoked bombardment of Copenhagen and sinking of the Danish fleet. But Danish circles in London reassured her that the Massy-Beresfords were a family of stature. "Bedstemoder," as Jorgen's mother was affectionately called by her children, gave them her blessing. So eventually did Monica's father. Jorgen's sound financial situation was in his favor, for George's unsuccessful exploration of American goldfields had substantially depleted the Massy-Beresford fortunes. A marriage settlement was drawn up in which a considerable sum of money was settled on Monica's children-to-be by her ever-generous mother. Jorgen, who could not legally break the entail on his estate, put in the value of his life-insurance policy and committed himself to future donations in cash.

They were married in London on June 15, 1916, at St. Margaret's Church, a quiet wedding in view of the critical times and dismal news from the battlefields. The London press devoted columns to the list of distinguished guests arriving from Denmark, to the bride's and bridesmaids' dresses, and to the fact that the Primate of Ireland had traveled to England especially to officiate at the wedding. Braving German U-boats, Axel Wichfeld arrived from the United States to be best man for his brother. Addi, the youngest sister, was a bridesmaid; Tim and Jack, both on leave from the front, escorted their mother to church "and sang hymns in Danish with gusto." The couple went to Brighton for their honeymoon, where, surprisingly, Monica's brother Jack joined them for a few days (neither Monica nor Jorgen seemed to mind). On their return to London, they moved into a large sunny flat in Egerton Crescent, one of London's most fashionable addresses, hired a cook, butler, and lady's maid and settled down. Monica's married life had begun.

*   *   *

The four years that followed were outwardly very happy. Jorgen was an affectionate and generous husband; they were surrounded by friends, entertained lavishly, and Monica was free to indulge her passion for decorating her new home. Money seemed to be plentiful for Jorgen, and he spent a substantial amount in transforming his young Irish wife into an elegant society woman. Like Pygmalion, the sculptor in the legend, Jorgen Wichfeld delighted in bringing about her metamorphosis. Monica's Irish dressmakers and their homely creations were promptly banished in favor of Worth and Paris couture. Her thick dark hair, now cared for by the best London hairdressers, was at Jorgen's suggestion parted in the middle, pulled back into an elegant knot at the nape of the neck, and fastened by diamond or tortoiseshell combs. Although this hairdo made her look older than her years, it gave a distinctly classical shape to her face. She retained this style for the rest of her life. It set her apart from other women during the short-cropped fashions of the twenties and the loose shoulder-length styles of the thirties and forties. When Monica was a young girl, a strict governess had made her walk with a pitcher of water on her head and a broomstick across her back, tucked under her arms. This achieved the desired effect of an erect bearing, and an air of pride in the turn of the head. Jorgen had long observed that his wife, without being a raving natural beauty, had the rare gift some women possess of giving the impression of beauty. He set about to enhance her finer points and his efforts had the desired effect. Monica's sternest critic, her brother Tim, noted after visiting them: "I confess with amazement that, whereas in her early youth my sister used to be quite plain, with a somewhat lumpy figure, by the time she had been married a few years and was firmly established in London, she had changed into a remarkably handsome woman, well dressed, with a slim figure and surprisingly elegant legs—someone in fact that people looked at with undisguised admiration." When complimented on the change in his wife's looks, Jorgen smiled and went off to buy her another piece of jewelry.

They moved in an international circle of friends. In the last year of the war, not unlike similar days during World War II, foreigners flocked to London in droves, and many found their way to the cosmopolitan Wichfeld drawing room. "At most of their parties half a dozen foreign languages would be heard," recalled her intensely English brother Tim. "My sister's unique kind of charm attracted all sorts: actors, Russian emigrés, Belgians who had fled their country after it had been invaded, and assorted Americans sent over by Mabelle and Axel Wichfeld." At her parties Monica liked to sit quietly curled up on a sofa, listening to the talk whirling around her and adding a helpful or witty word. She and her salon became immensely popular. To her family and friends she appeared at peace and contented. Only her brother Jack, the person closest to her, detected an occasional note of dissatisfaction. "You seem to be leading a splendid life," he wrote his sister after one of his infrequent visits from the front. "I like Jorgen, I *hope* he is everything you have ever wanted." Jack knew Monica very well and was sensitive enough to realize that after two years of marriage his vital and now sexually awakened sister expected more from her husband than generosity, kindness, and mere companionship.

In the spring of 1918 a new German offensive against the combined British and French forces began. Again the front was established east of Ypres. In what was later described as the most bloody fighting of the entire war, the British forces lost over 125,000 men, and Sir Douglas Haig, the commander of the British armies, had to call in the last reserves. Only a few months before, Monica's brothers had both returned from France and been assigned to duty on the home front. Tim had contracted thrombosis in his left leg and Jack had had two fingers of his right hand smashed by enemy shrapnel. Now they both volunteered to report back to France. The Massy-Beresfords were distraught, and to avoid what she called "gloomy farewell rites," Monica and Jorgen arranged a weekend party in Hampshire with their new friends, the multimillionaire Belgian banker Alfred Loewenstein and his pretty French wife, Madeleine. It was not what Alice Massy-Beresford had hoped for; she would have preferred to have the boys to herself, but it was what Monica wanted. She dreaded Jack's departure for the front; it would be easier not to think about it over a cheerful weekend.

It was June, the weather was glorious, and Jack was in a boisterous mood in spite of his injuries. His blond hair bleached by the sun, his brown eyes smiling, he joked about "the delights of spending my impending twenty-first birthday in a foxhole in the trenches." They all returned to London on Sunday night and the two brothers boarded the train at Victoria, crossing over to France. It was the last time Monica ever saw Jack.

Tim won the Military Cross and was promoted to captain in the Rifle Brigade in July 1918, during the second Battle of the Marne. Young Jack became a full lieutenant and he too was decorated for valor. During the last week in August, the blow fell. Monica and Jorgen were getting ready to join friends for a concert at the Albert Hall. "I was sitting in front of my dressing table when in the mirror I saw Rosie, the Irish maid I had brought over from St. Hubert's, come into my room with a telegram in her hand," Monica told her son years later. "We all dreaded telegrams in those days. It said: 'Regret to tell you Jack dead . . . very quick . . . love from Mother.' "

Monica never truly recovered from the shock. She later explained to her son that she felt suddenly isolated, deprived of her "alter ego," the one person with whom she could communicate, practically by osmosis. She knew that no one could ever replace him and that no one could help her in her grief. Her husband? It would have been different perhaps had they been a close-knit, intimate couple; Jorgen was instantly supportive and "infinitely kind," she recalled. Yet she could not bring herself to talk to him about Jack, or to her family, for that matter; she shared their grief, but she refused to discuss him. Her mother found consolation in deep religious faith, but Jack's death turned Monica into an agnostic. She could not accept "a cruel and avenging God." Years later she even turned the religious education of her children over to her mother and to their Italian governess Olga, saying that she did not want to influence them with her feelings. It also made her passionately anti-German. She, who had loved her time in Dresden and was proud of her proficiency in the language, now could not bear to hear a word of German spoken; she blamed the entire nation for her loss. In years to come, she refused to visit Germany except in transit, and had no German friends except one, whom fate's supreme irony put in her path shortly after her arrival in Denmark. In the days of World War II, the memory of Jack's death on the battlefield became the mainspring of Monica's heroism.

Life had to go on, though there seemed to be no end to gloomy news in the last few months before the Armistice.

Monica and Jorgen went over to St. Hubert's to be with her parents and on their way back to London heard that the Irish mail boat on which they had traveled the day before had been torpedoed with a number of their friends on board. "It was the most dreadful autumn," Monica's mother remembered. "It never stopped raining, grain had been rotting in the fields, and hardly a day passed without a friend or relative reported missing." After the Germans' final offensive thrust, the four-year nightmare came to a close on November 11. As soon as it was possible to travel, Monica went over to France to visit Jack's grave in the military cemetery in Bethancourt. She was expecting a baby—the future heir to Engestofte that Jorgen wanted—but her depression continued. Her mother, worried by her daughter's continued low spirits, hoped that the new arrival would help her to come to terms with Jack's death. "Her grief is so immense that we all feel powerless to help her," she wrote.

Early in the new year Monica became ill with the flu, which in the aftermath of the war raged on the Continent and in England. It took her a long time to recover, her depression making her condition much worse. In early 1919, the Wichfelds moved to a house in Thurloe Square in Kensington. It was a comfortable Victorian four-story building, light and roomy, with a large garden overlooking a leafy square. The living room with its triple bay window was filled with sunshine, and on the first morning in her new home Monica felt her spirits revive. Three weeks later her son Ivan was born, a strong, healthy baby of unmistakable Nordic appearance. With Ivan's birth, Monica recovered her peace of mind and her physical health. She insisted on nursing the baby herself; she even took him to France when again she went to visit

Jack's grave. Gradually, as the demands on Monica's time intensified, the heir to Engestofte was handed over to the care of an excellent nanny summoned from Denmark.

In the two years following the war, the Wichfelds led a life of intense social activity. The London to which the combatants returned after they took off their uniforms and laid down their arms was not the bombed-out, blacked-out, food-rationed capital that survived World War II. There was no physical damage to speak of and, though there were inevitable social changes, the basic structure of prewar society remained relatively unchanged. To those whose luck had held and who emerged alive from the trenches, enjoyment seemed a well-earned right. Jorgen and Monica joined in the parties. Her well-kept albums of photographs record weekends in an assortment of grand country houses, trips to Paris for days at a time, visits to the cinema and the theater (they saw *The Second Mrs. Tanqueray* with Gladys Cooper twice), races at Ascot and Newmarket, and of course frequent forays to Lough Erne and Ireland. Monica's elegance and conversational gifts and Jorgen's proficiency at tennis and bridge kept them very much in demand. They rarely spent an evening at home together, and in this they were no different from other social young couples of their day. In this period they also became famous for their dancing.

Every age has its fashionable pursuits and after the war dancing and ballet and, to a lesser extent, tennis and bridge became the rage. It was as if people were seeking the mildest of pastimes after a long period of violence. Pavlova, Karsavina, Nijinsky, Adele and Fred Astaire, and Irene and Vernon Castle were the popular idols. The great operatic bass Chaliapin, majestic in stature and as celebrated a lover as he was a singer, personified the land from which the sublime Russian ballets had come. He pursued Monica after one of his recitals at Queen's Hall, but was soon whisked away by the dazzling Lady Diana Cooper.

The Wichfelds were very much in tune with their generation. They could hold their own in all the fashionable pursuits, but what they really excelled at was dancing. Monica's grace and skill were often compared with that of the famous Mrs. Vernon Castle, the rage of the 1920s. The Embassy Club in Bond Street, with Luigi's band, was the regular society haunt at the time; on most nights the Prince of Wales could be seen with his party at a table by the dance floor. The Wichfelds spent many evenings at the Embassy, among the proprietor's favorite guests. On most occasions, whenever they took the floor, people would stop dancing to watch them and applaud. Of average height, they both moved like a single person, with effortless grace and confidence. They held themselves erect, gliding across the floor with faultless rhythm, the upper part of their bodies motionless. No doubt this talent they both possessed must have been a great bond between them: it had brought them together in the first place. Their children recall that there often used to be dancing after dinner at Engestofte. Monica always took particular pleasure instructing them and imparting her gifts to the young.

To add even more glamour to the scene, Axel and Mabelle Wichfeld came over from America, determined to give themselves and their family a good time. Jorgen's younger brother was then twenty-eight and well known for his good looks and mischievous charm. As the estate of Engestofte was entailed, with Jorgen sole heir, Axel had been sent to America to make his own way in the world. Intelligent and very able, he was well on the way to becoming a successful banker when he met Mabelle Moore, widow of financier Clarence Moore, who had gone down with the *Titanic*. Her father, Edwin C. Swift, had brought his only daughter up to believe that she need never worry about money. When she met Axel Wichfeld in Wilmington, Delaware, at the Du Ponts', she decided that he too must be hers and promptly proposed to him. The prospect of marrying a woman whose income was more than a million dollars a year—a staggering sum in the twenties— was more than Axel could resist. He abandoned his banking career, married Mabelle, and from then on devoted his life to the pursuit of pleasure. Six years older than Axel and very much in love with him, Mabelle wished to give him as agreeable a life as possible. As Axel enjoyed being in Europe, she immediately bought him an eighteenth-century *hôtel particulier* on the Left Bank in Paris. They also maintained suites at both the Paris and the London Ritz, and proceeded to rent sporting estates in England and Scotland to assure the best shooting and fishing for themselves and their many friends. Generous by nature, Mabelle lived on a truly grand scale. She thought nothing of hiring special trains, fleets of Rolls-Royces, and armies of servants to make life easy and agreeable. Passionately interested in jewelry and clothes, she collected the most expensive Paris models and always traveled with a truckload of Vuitton trunks that contained her personal silver, bed and table linen, as well as her enormous wardrobe. Her laundry was flown to Belgium by special plane, for she claimed that only in a particular convent in Bruges was it done to her satisfaction.

Though Mabelle led a superficial and restless life and her extravagances were legendary, she was essentially a good and simple person and could be a devoted friend. Monica found her sister-in-law sensitive and "rather vulnerable," a description not often before applied to the heiress. A strong friendship developed between the rich middle-aged woman and her young relative by marriage. It lasted for over ten years, until Mabelle's death in 1933, caused by worry in the aftermath of the Wall Street crash. But in the twenties, in Denmark or in England, they often spent hours together curled up on a sofa talking. There was an unexpected benefit in it for Monica: as Mabelle never wore a dress more than once and fur coats for only a season, many of her splendid couturier creations, suitably altered, ended up in Monica's clothes closets. Jolly and comfortably fat, Mabelle enjoyed seeing them on her slender sister-in-law.

For over three years after the end of the war, Jorgen continued with his work at the Danish legation. He was not a qualified or trained diplomat, like the rest of the staff, and his duties were not onerous. In the early twenties, however, new Danish state regulations came into force, restricting employment to career officers in the service. Jorgen had felt for some time that the moment was approaching when the family ought to return to Denmark. Monica was expecting another baby and his mother wished it to be born at Engestofte. (Their daughter, Varinka, was born there on February 9, 1922.) This latest development forced his hand. The house in Thurloe Square was given up, trunks of all sizes and shapes were filled with Monica's trousseau and their innumerable possessions, tiny Ivan was equipped with an assortment of clothes to protect him from the Arctic cold of the North. Monica bought a lynx-lined leather country jacket, and after an endless succession of parties and tearful farewells from their friends, they sailed across the North Sea from Hull to Copenhagen and then to Lolland.

Shortly before their departure Monica exchanged her

comfortable British passport, with its jovial lion and unicorn, and its requirement in the name of His Britannic Majesty that she be afforded every protection, for the blue-and-black passport issued by the Kingdom of Denmark, her new country, for which she was to give her life twenty years later.

Three

House on the Lake

THE BALTIC is a northern sea, brilliant blue in sunlight, murky gray in fog and rain, and deep gold on summer afternoons at sunset, when it turns to the color of amber seen only in these waters. On its northern coasts, bordering Sweden and Denmark, the Baltic is fringed with pine forests, fjords, pebble beaches, and myriads of tiny islands. Its southern shore, along Poland, Finland, and Russia, is gentler, lined with white sandy beaches, dunes, marshes, and low mud cliffs behind which grow fields of wild myrtle bushes and gorse. Long stretches are edged with shoals, sand spits, and wide shallow lagoons. Four great rivers make their way to the Baltic—the Neva, the Dvina, the Vistula, and the Oder, pouring fresh water into the sea so that the prevailing current flows out. Due to this geological freak, it is difficult for salt water to enter the Baltic and the lack of salt brings ice. Winter comes early, often in late October, with heavy frost and flurries of snow. In the days of sailing ships, Baltic captains steered their ships into port, unrigged them, and left the hulls locked in the ice until spring. The Baltic comes to life once more in spring, and during the short summer it is crisscrossed by vessels from every country in the world.

The islands of Lolland and Falster, flat, fertile, and thickly wooded, stretch along the southern tip of Denmark. In Monica's day their only link with the outside world was the ferries carrying rail and road traffic north to Copenhagen and south to the German port of Warnemünde, from which roads led to Berlin. In the 1930s what was then the longest bridge in the world was built between the islands and the mainland. But when Monica came there, the islands were a remote and self-contained world whose people seldom traveled; they used a local dialect from the time of the Vikings. In most villages water was still pumped by hand. Apart from the rare motorcar, transport was by horsecart, bicycle, or foot. Wood-burning stoves provided heat, electricity had just started to be installed, telephones were rare. On Lolland there were only two small towns—Maribo and Nykøbing—medieval in character, with cobbled streets, stone buildings, high-pitched roofs and gables.

When Monica arrived to claim possession of her new home, she was met at the ferry by an old Ford station wagon and driven past the town of Maribo and the watermill, on through woods full of wildflowers and plane trees. A driveway lined with majestic elm and lime trees led to the graceful, low-slung, ocher-colored house, and beyond it was the lake, stretching for miles. On the gravel sweep to the portico stood their agent and steward, Christian Kann, to welcome the lady of Engestofte to her new home.

A few days before, following an age-long tradition, her mother-in-law, Bedstemoder, had moved out to make room for her eldest son's wife. Taking her young daughter Addi and the majority of house servants with her, she installed herself at a small estate called Troldebjerg, fifty miles away on Falster, where she remained the rest of her life. The rules of inheritance in those days were harsh, but Bedstemoder was luckier than many: Jorgen was only twenty-two when his father died; for the next fourteen years, while he traveled and lived in London, she ruled over Engestofte, an old-fashioned woman of stern Victorian principles. Monica's brother Tim remembered her as "a formidable and querulous lady, with piercing blue eyes, very red complexion, and a mustache, who had always dominated J whenever they happened to be under the same roof."

Engestofte had been the seat of the Wichfeld family for generations. In 1727 Bertel Wichmand, a rich merchant from Falster, bought the estate and was succeeded by his son Jorgen. When in 1776 Jorgen bought the neighboring estate of Ulrichsdaal, Christian VII granted him a patent of nobility with the name von Wichfeld. In 1797, during the French Revolution, Jorgen Wichfeld left the entire estate to his nephew Henning on condition that it be entailed in perpetuity to the eldest male heir. Young Henning, an attractive and able army officer, commissioned an architect, probably Italian, to build him a new seat in the fashionable neoclassical style, surrounded by acres of parkland. Henning von Wichfeld was a well-traveled man, and his wife was a talented painter. They were close friends of the renowned Danish sculptor Thorvaldsen, who often stopped at Engestofte when not living at his home in Rome. When Henning's son succeeded to the estate, Engestofte had its golden period. His wife, Varinka, twenty-two years younger than her husband, came from the distinguished Rosenkrantz family of *Hamlet* fame. She was the niece and heiress of Niels Rosenkrantz, a celebrated Danish prime minister and former ambassador to St. Petersburg. Varinka Wichfeld was a successful painter, but she was also well educated, witty, and had great conversational gifts. She befriended writers and poets at Engestofte during the summer and entertained at her salon in Copenhagen during the long Northern winters; she was called "the Danish Madame de Staël." Varinka Wichfeld was also extremely rich, having inherited a huge fortune and splendid jewels from a Russian aunt, as well as lovely furniture of Russian blond birchwood in English Chippendale style. By now the house had forty rooms and a hundred windows, most of the downstairs drawing rooms opening one into the other. Varinka built terraces going down to the lake, made formal gardens, restored two estate churches, and built two old people's homes for estate workers. Inordinately proud of her lineage, she had the local tradesmen bring their wares to her carriage, Russian fashion. Her husband was made chamberlain to Christian IX, and her two unmarried daughters, who did not inherit their mother's looks, became ladies-in-waiting to the queen. Varinka's son, another Henning, who succeeded in 1888, was Jorgen de Wichfeld's father and Monica's late father-in-law.

Monica found that the old Empire decorations were hidden under layers of dark brown Victorian wallpaper introduced by Bedstemoder, but the doors still retained their ivory paint and fine gilding. Having been continuously lived in for over a century and a half, the house was full of reminders of an earlier age—drawings and paintings by Varinka and her predecessors, eighteenth-century silver, Russian porcelain and glass that came with Varinka's dowry, cupboards bursting with embroidered linen, and pottery painted by assorted aunts and great-aunts. Often Monica opened a drawer to find an eighteenth-century purse or a pair of ancient spectacles in

their original case; daily the house yielded up hidden me-
mentos.

Engestofte's unique charm was due to its lovely position.
It faced south, and all the main rooms were on that side,
facing the lake. The high windows let in the light and the
sun; on the floor above, the main bedrooms also overlooked
the lake through the crowns of the old lime trees. The northern
side of the house contained a neoclassical hall with Thorvaldsen roundels; there was access to two staircases and more
bedrooms. In front a terrace with stone steps led to a lower
garden, a Chinese pavilion built over a natural spring, and a
small private pier on the lake. Beyond this stretched an unbroken vista—two miles of gray-blue water with not a building
or even a telegraph pole in sight. It was like living in a private
world of one's own.

The lake cast its spell over the house. It was different
from Lough Erne, because it was enhanced by the dramatic
changes in the seasons. From the first day in her new home,
Monica felt its spell. "Fate must have wished," Alice Massy-
Beresford remarked, when she came to visit her daughter that
Christmas, "that my child's destiny should unfold between
two Northern lakes."

It was a daunting task for a young English girl to find
herself the mistress of a feudal estate in a remote corner of
Denmark. She had tried to learn Danish while in London—
Jorgen had even engaged a private tutor—but somehow there
never had been enough time for the lessons. And Jorgen was
not much help; it was years since he had lived in Denmark;
running the place bored him. He wanted a beautiful, comfortable home that would satisfy his aesthetic requirements
and do justice to his position in the county. He liked garden-

ing, knew a great deal about plants, and filling the house with flower arrangements occupied a large amount of his time. Monica realized that the first order of business was to learn Danish. A schoolteacher was recruited from Maribo; he used to bicycle to the house every morning.

He also doubled as translator and adviser on hiring painters, carpenters, plumbers, and indoor staff. Monica had the heavy Victorian wallpapers stripped and replaced with pastel paints, the Empire decorations revived, the furniture rearranged and recovered in light colors, and additional bathrooms installed. A new regime of light, cheerfulness, and fresh paint was ushered in. "Doing up houses" was Monica's special talent; Nancy Lancaster, a famous English decorator, remembered being impressed by Monica's instinctive knowledge of proportions and her flair for color, the more remarkable since she never had any formal training in the field.

Once the house had been made agreeable to live in, the Wichfelds embarked on a tour of visits in the neighborhood. The first place on the list was Aalholm, home of the Raben family, a storybook castle complete with moat, towers, turrets, and an immense park where deer grazed among oak trees planted in the Middle Ages. Countess Raben, who presided over a household of feudal splendor, was an old friend of the Wichfeld family; she had been educated in England and gone to the same boarding school as Monica's mother. Her daughter Suzanne, a gifted illustrator and short-story writer, was to become one of Monica's closest friends. There were also the Rosenørn-Lehns, who lived in a lovely house on the Baltic with front lawns going down to the sea; the Bertouch-Lehns at Lungholm; and the distinguished family of Count Frijs, whose cousin Baroness Blixen, ten years older than Monica, was living on her farm in Kenya.

Known by her writing name, Isak Dinesen, she and Monica were to meet on her return to Denmark some years later. There was only one family she absolutely refused to see: the Haugwitz-Reventlow brothers at Hardenberg Castle, Engestofte's nearest neighbors. Notwithstanding their respectable Danish title and age-long residence in Denmark, they were German. What made it worse was that Kurt, the younger brother, had been an officer in the German army during the war and only recently had returned to farm in Denmark. To Monica they were the enemies responsible for the death of her beloved brother Jack; no amount of persuasion would induce her to call on them.

It made for an awkward situation. Heini, the older brother, was a friend of Jorgen's from childhood. Lean, wry, and balding, with a languid self-assurance that concealed a sharp and somewhat Machiavellian mind, Heini Reventlow had inherited one of the largest and most beautiful estates in Denmark. Hardenberg was a romantic moated castle set in a perfectly planned eighteenth-century park. Hans Christian Andersen wrote *The Ugly Duckling* at Hardenberg, while staying in the Chinese pavilion on an island in one of the estate's small lakes. This huge property bordered on Engestofte and was almost twice its size.

One day in late summer the two brothers decided to ride over to Engestofte to see what was going on. Monica's personality and looks were beginning to have an impact on the island society, and the changes she wrought on the hitherto gloomy house had become the subject of animated comments. Heini, who had always looked upon Jorgen as a confirmed bachelor like himself, was curious to meet his friend's reputedly fascinating English bride. From her bedroom window on the first floor, Monica saw the two handsome figures alight, hand over the reins of their mounts to the groom, and confidently address the butler in the hall. She sent word that she was not at home to receive them.

As time went on, however, it became obvious that such an attitude would be impossible to keep up in a small, closed society consisting of about a dozen families used to entertaining each other. Jorgen and Heini were contemporaries. It was Kurt, slightly younger than Monica, who attracted her, however. They inevitably met again and again at picnics, bathing parties, tennis games, shooting matches, and weekend parties. Monica remained aloof and fought hard against an unexpected physical attraction to a man whom she still thought of as an enemy. But gradually her hostility collapsed and she came to appreciate her neighbor's friendliness and sensational looks. Finally, her capitulation was complete: they fell in love with each other.

How did this state of affairs come about? Why did Jorgen not prevail as her husband and the father of their children, and how did Monica come to terms with her virulent anti-German feelings? She would have been the first to admit that it was hard to explain, but a picture of her state of mind emerges from her brother Tim's reminiscences and the talks she had years later with her son Viggo. At the time of her meeting with Kurt, Monica was twenty-seven years old and at the height of her beauty. Because of the sophisticated circles in which they moved, she had become a worldly and elegant woman, famed for her wit and powers of fascination. People sooner or later fell under her spell; the family's phrase for it was "being attached to her chariot wheels." In spite of the admiration she evoked, however, Monica seemed to be restless and lonely. Since the early days of her marriage it had been apparent to those nearest to her that her relationship with her husband lacked the vitality and excitement her Irish temperament demanded. Jorgen was a devoted, civilized companion, an aesthete with impeccable manners and taste. At thirty-eight, he appeared to attach little importance to the physical aspects of love. And suddenly here was Kurt, twelve years younger than Jorgen, bursting with vibrant youth, remarkably good-looking, who ardently admired Monica and was constantly in her presence.

Kurt dashed about in a yellow, two-seated Hudson; he dressed carelessly in slightly raffish country tweeds, adored jazz music, and was a magnificent sportsman. Highly intelligent and active, he had a strong streak of recklessness that struck a chord in Monica. It is not hard to imagine Kurt's appeal to Monica in comparison with the somewhat precious Jorgen, with his perfectly cut London suits, slow, precise speech, and eternal monocle on a string. He was agreeable to be with but, unlike Kurt, totally ineffectual as a partner or counselor in the daily running of the estate.

The attraction that Monica held for Kurt, apart from her physical beauty and sparkle—"I desired her the moment I laid eyes on her," he confessed to his old friend Clara Hasselbach—was probably her worldliness and social polish. Kurt's experience of women had been mostly casual affairs with actresses in Copenhagen, farm girls on his cousin's German estates in Silesia, or brief encounters while on leave from the army. He had never met a woman like Monica, who attracted him physically and was at the same time a *femme du monde*—unattainable unless he succeeded in wooing her. Whatever the underlying reasons, the attraction was genuine and intense, and circumstances played into their hands. In the tight world of the island they were constantly thrown together.

Kurt had just taken over the lease of one of his brother's farms with a small manor house called Rosenlund, barely two miles from Engestofte. He asked Monica to help him decorate his new residence, which until then had been lived in by a tenant farmer and needed everything done to it. Monica responded with enthusiasm, and within a few months the house was transformed into a sunny, charming, well-heated replica of an English country home, with comfortable sofas, cheerful colors, and bowls of flowers everywhere, in marked contrast to the heavy Germanic interiors of their neighbors. Kurt was delighted, and soon they were seeing each other almost daily. Kurt, whose English was a bit sketchy, undertook to improve Monica's Danish; she in turn always addressed him in English. Ever bent on improving people, she taught him to play bridge, put him in touch with her London stockbroker, even recommended Jorgen's Savile Row tailors. Life took on a different hue for Monica. For the first time since childhood, she felt truly herself. She was happy.

Heini, who watched with wry amusement the growing closeness between his brother and his old friend's wife, now decided to give a Venetian fête at Hardenberg for Monica. Boats with lanterns glided on the ponds and canals under the castle walls, and bands played. Guests who had come from all over Scandinavia promenaded under the trees in the soft twilight of a Northern evening. Monica wore a yellow pleated Fortuny dress with a belt sewn with brilliants and a diamond necklace around her neck. She looked stunning; Kurt never left her side throughout the evening. And Jorgen? Faultlessly dressed and aloof, he surveyed the scene through his monocle with a benevolent expression on his face, delighted at his wife's success. It was as if the approval of his friends and neighbors was also a tribute to him.

The summer after Monica's arrival at Engestofte was unusually hot for Denmark. There had been very little rain and the level of the lake in front of the house had fallen so low that for the first time in memory mud islands with traces of prehistoric settlements came into view. The harvest was being brought in and the threshing machine was busily working on the farm. Jorgen had gone to Copenhagen to consult with his lawyer and banker about his financial situation. Because of new government legislation, it had unexpectedly taken a turn for the worse. Monica was alone at Engestofte with her small son and baby daughter. One afternoon she was sitting on the floor in the library sorting out crates of books which had recently come from London. As she leafed through a heavy tome, she noticed a dark patch on a page and, thinking it might have got damp during transport, she brushed the page with the back of her hand. The spot moved; then another patch appeared and floated downward. Puzzled, she looked up at the three north windows and saw that ashes were raining down outside. A moment later a herd of cows came stampeding past the windows, maddened with fear.

She rushed into the hall and opened the massive front door. There was a strong east wind and an ominous glow behind the kitchen wing. On the terrace she could see that the thatched roof of the long barn and the cowshed were engulfed in flames and that the wind was blowing the flames toward the stables and the main house. Farm workers were running up the drive carrying smoldering furniture and belongings, while a shower of cinders covered everything like black snow. She tried to tell the farm workers not to leave the furniture so dangerously close to the house, but her Danish was inadequate. Someone had summoned the fire brigade, but their hoses were too short to reach the water in the lake, which because of the drought had retreated hundreds of yards from the shore. Monica sent the children and the nurse to the safety of the park and telephoned Kurt. He arrived ten minutes later and took charge.

The fire had been started by a spark from the threshing machine and had spread to bales of dry straw. The cows had all been released, but the bulls were trapped in their pens and some of the large cart horses, terrified by the flames, refused to move. Kurt quickly organized a chain of farm workers with buckets to transport water by hand from the lake and pour it onto the roofs of the remaining buildings. Monica stood on the lawn watching Kurt, his figure lit by the glow of the flames, directing the rescue operation. His face was blackened and rivulets of perspiration were running down; he occasionally staggered onto the terrace to snatch a mug of beer and then rushed back to join the others beating the flames with spades and trampling them with heavy boots.

Returning from Copenhagen and crossing over to Lolland, Jorgen noticed the red glow in the distance, but it was only when he reached Maribo that he realized it was his own farm burning. By the time he reached Engestofte, the fire had been contained and Kurt was the hero of the day. Next morning they inspected the smoking ruins. An acrid smell of burned flesh, dead cattle, and blackened straw hung over the entire area. Jorgen stared in bemused silence at the devastation. The sudden loss of the main farm with its annual harvest was a grave financial setback, but the fire was only the latest in a series of financial misfortunes brought about by Jorgen's irresponsibility and the new socialist legislation in Denmark. Realizing that her husband was unable to cope, and determined to protect her small children, Monica gathered the reins of administration in her own hands and turned for advice to her lover.

The unexpected collapse of the Wichfeld family finances came as a bolt from the blue. One day Monica was the wife of a rich landowner, mistress of a beautiful house, attended by a large staff of servants; the next day creditors were beating at her door. Many factors were beyond her husband's control, but the main fault undoubtedly lay with him. Jorgen de Wichfeld succeeded to his father's estate at twenty-two. In the next fifteen years, which included his travels, his marriage to Monica, and their opulent existence in London, he communicated with his bank or with his farm steward only when he needed money. Being a generous man, he showered presents on his friends and his young wife. Hardly a day passed without his returning from work at the legation in London with a piece of jewelry, a cigarette case, or something discovered in a London antique shop. Monica always possessed the visible accessories of a rich woman, *les signes extérieures de la richesse*, such as exquisite cigarette holders, golden compacts, splendid purses and furs. These presents, together with theater tickets, tailors' bills, and couturier clothes were always charged to Jorgen's account on the assumption that the bills would be transmitted to Denmark and paid by his bank and estate. Houses were rented in the most fashionable parts of London, a sizable staff was brought over by Monica from Ireland, their parties and travels were lavish. Monica and her parents believed that Jorgen was a very rich man able to support such a life-style. Jorgen thought so too. Had he taken the trouble to inquire about what was going on back home, he would have

discovered that his agent, instead of settling current bills for
fertilizer, seed, fencing posts, and the countless items essential
to running a farm, was sending the money to Jorgen's credit
rather than paying steadily accumulating debts. No dishonesty
was involved. Several letters to Jorgen explained the facts, but
he either did not understand or did not want to. Always extremely well off, he had acquired the habits and attitudes of
the very rich. It had never occurred to him that he might be
hopelessly overdrawn.

Monica learned of what was happening by sheer chance.
On the main square of Maribo stood an old-fashioned grocery
store called Qvade's. It had a dual function: in addition to its
retail business in the front, it supplied seed and fertilizer to
all the big estates on Lolland and carried on a thriving whole-
sale business as a grain merchant. One day Monica stopped
at Qvade's to buy some toothpaste. When the clerk asked
whether to add the toothpaste to their bill, she declined and
said she would rather pay cash. She then asked to see the
outstanding account. The clerk seemed taken aback and summoned the manager, who bowed and said it would take some
time to prepare. Monica thought this odd and drove back to
Engestofte, but forgot about it.

Ten days later the bill arrived. As it was addressed to her,
Monica opened it and could not believe what she saw: it
included all the fertilizer, seed, ironmongery, wire, and a
multitude of items supplied to the estate over more than ten
years. After she had consulted with the steward, it became
painfully clear that there was no way this enormous bill could
be paid.

Qvade's bill was only the tip of the iceberg. Further in-
vestigations showed that for years they had been living on
credit in a fool's paradise. There were reasons why their in-

come had been drastically reduced: the Russian Revolution of 1917 had rendered valueless the stocks and bonds the Wichfelds had inherited from their rich Russian grandmother's estate; the postwar depression had caused a slump in farm prices after the very profitable war years; the law passed late in 1921 by the socialist government forced entailed estates like Engestofte to surrender 25 percent of their land and a fifth of their capital to the state. The levy was a nasty blow and everyone grumbled about it, but the majority managed to pay and retain their estates. Jorgen's neighbors on Lolland had set aside capital during boom times. Needless to say, no capital had been set aside by Jorgen for such an eventuality. Loans from banks had reached a point where the estate could no longer meet interest payments. The original 1777 entailment specified that a certain capital sum had to be set aside for the next male heir, but the mortgaged value of the estate did not cover this sum. Public trustees had to be called in. That was why Jorgen had gone to Copenhagen.

Monica and Kurt did what they could to satisfy or fend off the small creditors who began to press their claims when word got around that the Engestofte finances were shaky. It was a desperate time for Monica. She would not have been able to cope without Kurt, the one solid rock in the quagmire of mismanagement, Jorgen's words of repentance, and the steward's explanations. Kurt was an experienced farmer who knew about modern agriculture; he saw to it that the damage from the fire was properly and promptly assessed, and he dealt with the insurance companies, which paid in full. There was more cash available for the most pressing creditors. Under Kurt's supervision, the work of rebuilding the farm was started. A tenant farmer was engaged, and by the following autumn modern red brick buildings were completed. Kurt divided his time between Rosenlund and Engestofte, running his own farm and at the same time advising Monica on restructuring the Wichfeld affairs. At the end of the day he would ride over, leave his mount in the stables, and bound up the terrace steps to the house, where Monica awaited him with a drink.

Sometimes they would drive off separately to meet in Copenhagen, Kurt in his yellow Hudson, Monica in her beloved old white convertible. With her white leather jacket, blue scarf flying in the wind, dark hair caught at the nape with a tortoiseshell barrette, Monica raced over the long straightaway stretch of the seashore exhilarated by the speed and sea breezes. Like a Scott Fitzgerald heroine, one of the "lost generation," she savored her fleeting moments of happiness with Kurt. Her worries receded into the background; she was young, in love, and had infinite faith in the future.

In spite of Kurt's efforts, his good advice, and the success of the newly reorganized farm, the public trustees decided that further economies were necessary to preserve the entailment. The obvious target of course was the family budget, since the management staff and some thirty estate workers and their families could not, according to the new legislation, be fired or have their salaries reduced. After consultation with accountants, it was decided to close the house during the six winter months to save on maintenance, heating bills, and household wages. Compared with the rest of Europe, the cost of living in Denmark was very high in those days. It would be cheaper for the family to go abroad until the situation became clearer.

That winter they went to Scotland as guests of Mabelle and Axel Wichfeld, who had rented Blair Castle near Perth for a season of pheasant shooting. Accompanied by the now inseparable Kurt, the Wichfelds traveled by boat to Newcastle, where Mabelle's chauffeur met them in a Rolls-Royce and drove them north. It was a welcome break for Monica. She looked forward to long intimate conversations with her favorite sister-in-law; much had happened since they had last seen each other.

The next year, in late spring, while Jorgen remained in Denmark with little Ivan, Monica and her small daughter Varinka (called Inkie) traveled to Ireland to spend some time with her parents. George Massy-Beresford's health was giving cause for concern and Monica wanted to help her mother. She herself had not been feeling well lately and was thinking of going to Dublin to consult her old family doctor. At Lough Erne, in her old room on one of the first warm days of the year, watching the noisy seagulls, Monica suspected that she was pregnant again. It was with mounting excitement that she set off for Dublin to see her doctor. The venerable family physician confirmed that she was expecting; the baby would be born in late December. Monica returned to St. Hubert's the next day to meet Kurt, who was arriving from London that evening. One wonders what her mother thought of Kurt's continuous presence at her daughter's side. The truth must have been apparent to her, as it had been for some time to Monica's brother Tim, now a full colonel, married, and living in England. But her father, whose health was failing at the time, certainly did not give it a thought. Haugwitz-Reventlow was to him just one more of Monica's Danish friends, a member of an illustrious family, one of the dozens of guests who continually streamed through St. Hubert's. George Massy-Beresford admired Kurt's excellent horsemanship and the way he handled the boats on Lough Erne. Of course he would have been deeply shocked had he known the facts, but his reaction would have been the same as his wife's: the marriage to Jorgen must be preserved at all costs. There would be no divorce in the family.

Leaving her daughter and the nurse at St. Hubert's, Monica returned to Denmark in late May. She found Jorgen suffering from a bad bronchial cold and deeply worried about their deteriorating finances. A meeting with the trustees, arranged after Monica's return, confirmed that further stringent economy measures would have to be taken. Between meetings with the trustees and coping with mountains of bills, the Wichfelds reviewed their personal situation. We shall never know precisely what passed between them, but according to an intimate friend of the couple, Jorgen was determined that their marriage should continue as before. He did not object to Kurt; he even welcomed him as a permanent fixture in the household. What he would not contemplate was life without Monica's support; she was his pillar of strength, the mother of his two children, a wonderful cheerful companion; he was utterly devoted to her and indeed loved her. As for Kurt, whom he had known all his life, it was easy to understand the attraction he held for Monica. Let him stay, if such was Monica's wish.

It was a generous response from a man who was essentially weak. Jorgen of course was deeply affected by the turn of events; it later contributed to his illness. His attitude evoked a wave of gratitude and affection in Monica. In spite of Reventlow's pressure for her to divorce Jorgen and marry him, she chose to remain with Jorgen. His need of her was overwhelming. As she later confessed, "I would not have been able to live with myself for the guilt." She chose a difficult path, one that eventually created the circumstances leading to her death. During the remaining twenty years of her life, she grew into a formidable personality, worshipped by her husband and her children. It was years before Kurt faded out of her life. By then she had spiritually and emotionally outgrown him, for she was in the service of a cause in which individual lives ceased to matter.

Four

Career Woman

MONICA'S FATHER died at St. Hubert's that July. The morning after his death, Monica's mother came down to breakfast and announced that she had decided to live in Italy. She had never liked Ireland and its climate. Now that she was not needed there any longer, she was anxious to return to the part of the world where she had been happy as a child. The place she chose to make her new home was Rapallo, the small seaside town near Genoa which used to be fashionable as a gambling resort before the war. In Italy the cost of living was cheap and the climate benign. She found a large, comfortable villa set back from the main road, with gardens front and back, a wonderful view of the sea and the promontory of Portofino in the distance. She named it Campo dei Fiori, in memory of her father's villa in Cannes. While details of the sale and money transfers were worked out, she divided her time between a house on Eaton Square in London and the house near Salisbury in Wiltshire where Tim and his family were living.

Engestofte had been closed since October and the Wichfelds were momentarily homeless. While Jorgen departed for a protracted stay in Switzerland to recover from his bronchial pneumonia, Monica and the children, after spending a month at Hardenberg with the Reventlow brothers, left for London. Her confinement was rapidly approaching and she was determined that her child be born in England, a British subject. A less overt reason was that it would probably be a good idea to be away from Danish gossip for a time. Viggo Dimitri de Wichfeld was born at 56 Eaton Square on the day after Christmas. He was a strong, perfectly formed little boy with clear blue eyes and a mop of reddish black hair. The birth had been easy and Monica recovered rapidly. According to her brother Tim's recollection, "She looked radiant."

A pattern of life now emerged that continued for the next seven years. The family spent late autumn, winter, and early spring in Italy or southern France, with occasional visits to England, returning to Engestofte in late April. In Italy as in France the exchange rate was very much in their favor, rented houses came cheaply, and servants were plentiful. In spite of their straitened circumstances, the Wichfelds managed to convey the impression of a well-off family escaping the climate of their native country.

Wherever they went Kurt followed, now accepted by all as a permanent member of the household. On their return from abroad each year, while Engestofte was made ready, Monica and the children spent a fortnight with Kurt at Rosenlund, his delightful farmhouse nearby. The same pattern was repeated in the autumn, while the house was being closed for the winter. This unusual arrangement naturally aroused comment in Denmark, but Monica, protected by the loyalty and devotion of her husband, paid no attention. In time the neighbors became used to the situation. "She is a law unto herself," her Danish friends used to say. Monica did indeed live her life according to her own code of behavior and her own concept of what was right. "I have made many mistakes," she told her son Viggo years later. "And I have sinned. But if I wanted something really badly and it was up to me to decide whether that wish should be fulfilled, I have always searched my soul and asked myself one question: 'Will I be harming anyone by doing this?' If the answer was *no*, I would ask again: 'Are you prepared to accept the retribution that will inevitably follow and face the criticism of your world, the kind of polite, whispered criticism that stops abruptly the moment one comes into the room? Am I prepared to see in the eyes of people I love the disapproval that they are too well-bred or too embarrassed to express?' If the answer to all these questions was a *yes*, I went ahead and did what I wanted. And later, when retribution arrived, I tried not to complain." Her sense of loyalty and her determination not to hurt anyone remained with her throughout her life. It explains why she never lost the devotion of her family and friends. To her children she was a wonderful mother; caring and loving and fun.

It could not have been a very satisfactory arrangement for Kurt. Friends still recall how deeply he was in love and how he repeatedly tried to convince Monica to leave Jorgen and marry him. But she invariably refused to discuss it; nor would she allow him to help her financially. Of the two, Jorgen needed her more and therefore she would remain by his side. No wonder Kurt used to "fly into rages." There were epic fights, break-ups, recriminations. He was a willful, passionate man, used to getting his own way. He wanted Monica for his wife and "to hell with everything else." His entreaties broke on the rock of Monica's determination, however; she loved him passionately in those days, but would not inflict irreparable damage on her family. "I knew that I would eventually lose him," she confessed to Clara Hasselbach, "but I couldn't have lived with myself if I had left Jorgen."

In looking through Monica's letters from the twenties, one becomes aware of a peculiar emptiness in her life during that period and wonders how someone of her acute intelligence and broad interests could have allowed herself to become a part of what would now be called the international café society set. Her photograph albums, redolent of the twenties, show her reclining on terraces of fashionable hotels in Italy and France, dressed in handmade couturier clothes, looking incredibly handsome in spite of the hideous fashions of the period, surrounded by Italian nobility, Russian princes, wealthy American expatriates; alighting from a Bugatti convertible in a palm-fringed courtyard at Cannes, escorted by the ever-present Kurt or by her husband. We see her dressed in impeccable shooting tweeds, standing in front of historic Blair Castle in Scotland, playing croquet on the lawn of some grand country house in England. One wonders how in their impoverished state the Wichfelds could afford the glamorous life, but they were a popular couple. Monica's clothes were given to her by her sister-in-law, and Jorgen's expenses were covered by the loan of a portfolio of shares from a devoted American family friend. The whole atmosphere in the twenties was one of "Let's enjoy life while we can," and Monica was not exactly immune to it. Her lovely face, shapely hands, splendid shoulders, and long jade cigarette holder are immortalized in her portrait by the Hungarian painter Meresz, it still adorns one of the reception rooms at Engestofte.

In England Monica knew everybody. She played tennis with Mrs. Winston Churchill, became a friend of Max Beaverbrook, whom she met at Lord Alington's, was taken to the theater by Noël Coward, dined in the company of Tallulah Bankhead, and lunched with Edwina Mountbatten. With her gift for spontaneous human contact she got on particularly well with Beaverbrook, who remained a staunch ally through the years. She recalled in a letter to her mother how they shared jokes about his amorous adventures. "And what did you do this afternoon?" asked Beaverbrook, coming up to Monica in the drawing room at Crichell, where they were both staying for the weekend. "Oh, I just rested and wrote letters," she answered. "How about you?" "I did too, but I had a pretty girl to tickle me—that's the difference." And they would both go off to play croquet, dissolved in laughter.

In Paris Mabelle and Axel Wichfeld reigned at 80 rue de Lille, their small, handsome, eighteenth-century palace (since demolished). Jorgen and Monica and their children had their own suite of rooms at Mabelle's and their own specially assigned butler and maid. They were Mabelle's most welcome and frequent guests, often staying for a month or six weeks. Invariably Kurt accompanied them.

In October 1929 the New York stock market crashed. It destroyed the fortunes of two sets of people who had been generously helping them over six difficult years, Mabelle and Axel Wichfeld and the Krebs family. All of a sudden Jorgen's brother and his millionairess wife were faced with financial collapse. Mabelle, always generous but extravagant and eccentric, had been gambling on the New York Stock Exchange, buying on margin, confident that her enormous fortune would protect her from undue risk. Soon after the market collapsed and she was on her way home on the *Bremen*, one of her Swift cousins committed suicide by jumping out of his office window. The rumor spread on Wall Street that the Swift empire was in financial straits. It was not true, but it caused an immediate and catastrophic drop in Swift shares, to the point where Mabelle's borrowings were no longer covered. Within the next twenty-four hours she was sold out. Having left Paris one of the richest women in the world, Mabelle, on her arrival in New York, found her fortune gone. During the remaining four years of her life (she died of pneumonia in London in February 1933), abandoned by her husband and most of her international fairweather friends, she spent her time selling off jewels, houses, cars, and her other possessions to pay her debts. Monica loyally stood by her; she refused forever after to see Axel, who went off and found himself another rich wife. Jorgen soon returned the almost worthless Krebs portfolio of shares to their owner, who needed them now as much as the Wichfelds. Lights were going out all over the fashionable spas. There was mounting unemployment, and vast debts. The party was at an end.

In the summer of 1930 Jorgen and Monica were at Engestofte once again, locked in discussions with their trustees. Both farms were now in the hands of tenants and the administrators were gradually paying off the crippling debts. These were lean times for Danish agriculture and the recovery process promised to be slow. The crash of 1929 had affected Monica's marriage settlement, and as Jorgen's income had almost completely dried up, they could no longer afford to spend the summer at Engestofte. The house would have to be let to raise money, and there was no other solution but to take advantage of Alice Massy-Beresford's generous offer to provide a home for them in her sprawling, comfortable villa at Rapallo. The cost of living in Italy was so low that Monica's mother could provide for them all and even employ six indoor servants and two gardeners. She adored her house and looked forward to the companionship of her grandchildren. But the children were growing up and school fees loomed; there were clothes and other expenses to cover. Jorgen's only excursion into business turned out to be a complete fiasco; for two or three months he actually had a job with an antique dealer in Paris. It was thought that his knowledge of French furniture, his excellent taste, and his circle of rich cosmopolitan friends would mean success, but as he later admitted, an entire month's salary disappeared during a session of drinks at the bar of the Paris Ritz, where he entertained acquaintances and friends, none of whom reciprocated by becoming a client. It fell to Monica to assume the role of family breadwinner; there was no other choice. She decided to try out her talents as a businesswoman.

Before she left Denmark that autumn, she had a final discussion with Kurt. Reventlow had been in her life for nine years. She still loved him, but their situation precluded a carefree relationship. It caused considerable strain on her part, and it was she who was beginning to get hurt. There had been acrimonious rows; Kurt was possessive and jealous and complained that Monica was "escaping him." This was not true, but as she developed self-confidence she was less and less vulnerable to his tantrums, though they took a heavy emotional toll. She had come to an important crossroad in her life: the future well-being of her children rested in her hands, she had to provide for their needs. Could she really go on with this relationship, and ought she not set Kurt free to find his own way, marry, and have his own children?

Having let the house at Engestofte, the entire family was staying with Kurt at Rosenlund. One morning Monica was alone typing lists on a small typewriter Kurt had given her because, as he claimed, her writing was impossible to decipher. It was early November, and outside, the lawns were white with frost. The front door banged and Kurt came in whistling a tune from a current London musical. Dressed in riding clothes, his face glowing with health and contentment, he threw himself into the armchair opposite and began to talk of their future. The time for decision had arrived; she must remain in Denmark with him. This was said in the tone of a military command and Monica felt something snap inside her. Quietly, without lifting her hands from the typewriter, she informed Kurt that it was all over between them, and went on typing her lists. He stared at her unbelievingly, changed the subject, and went out. But next morning, as the Wichfelds were leaving for Rapallo and trunks were being loaded, her eyes red after a sleepless night, Monica handed her lover a letter. It was goodbye. The relationship that had sustained her for nine years was over. As far as she was concerned, it belonged to the past.

Reventlow refused to take no for an answer and for years tried to re-establish contact. He followed her to Italy and to France, telephoned, sent flowers, and once, when he became too insistent, Monica sent a mutual friend to the Hôtel de Paris in Monte Carlo to convince him that her decision was indeed final. Their paths diverged. Kurt, whose farming had prospered, became very rich and developed a taste for the international *beau monde*. He was photographed skiing in St. Moritz, gambling in Monte Carlo, bathing at Cannes, and Monica often read about him in the papers. Their friendship was resumed for a time after Kurt's marriage to Barbara Hutton fell apart. The final break came only at the beginning of World War II, when Kurt, disregarding Monica's plea that he enlist in the Allied cause, decided to spend the war in America. (When he returned to Denmark six years later, his first move was to visit the church where a tablet to commemorate Monica's death had been erected.)

Monica now decided to embark on a business career, but her first task was to settle her husband and children in Rapallo. The Italian Riviera had been favored by English and North European travelers for centuries. Keats, one of the first poets to stay at Rapallo, described it as "magical." By the early 1920s, however, Rapallo had fallen behind other resorts, for the steep rise of the hills behind the town made its expansion impossible. Yet it remained a much favored retreat for artists and writers. Ezra Pound settled there in 1923 and shortly thereafter came Yeats. Hemingway came to visit, and on the terrace of the Albergo Rapallo one might meet Thomas Mann or Oscar Kokoschka. Max Beerbohm had a villa just outside town. A fashionable café, the Chuflay, was frequented by the American smart set, who played bridge and backgammon and escaped Prohibition. According to Yeats, both groups "met amiably at the town's tennis club." There were comparatively few tourists, "only those seeking tranquillity," as the local saying went.

Alice Massy-Beresford's villa, which lay just off the Roman Via Aurelia, was screened from the road by a hedge of scented whitethorn and tall iron gates. There was a walk of gray flagstones winding away beside a cypress hedge, and beyond it lay a small valley with a mountain torrent, a mill house with a pond, and fields sloping down to the sea. To the north, behind the kitchen garden, tier upon tier of olive-planted terraces rose up to the mountaintops. The peninsula of Portofino was clearly visible in the distance. The three-story square stucco house with green shutters was surrounded by mimosas, orange and lemon trees, and camellias. It was

spacious, comfortable, and pleasantly airy and it was Monica's
refuge for years. There was a devoted staff of Italian servants
who remained with the family all through World War II. As
Monica was away most of the time, the establishment in her
absence was run by Olga Signorini, a charming Italian spinster
whom Monica had met in Rapallo and persuaded to come to
live at the villa. She became an intimate friend and confidante
of Monica's and an adopted member of the Wichfeld and
Beresford families.

The last thing Alice Massy-Beresford had expected when
she bought her dream house in the sun was to share it one
day with her daughter and son-in-law and their three children. She ended up by thoroughly enjoying it. With its multiple bedrooms, terraces, and innumerable servants' rooms,
the villa was far too large for one person. The Wichfeld family
of two adults, three children, one governess, and Jorgen's
butler filled it nicely and provided the constant animation
it needed. Nor did the increased costs cause Alice Massy-
Beresford much worry, although in the wake of the Crash her
investments had dwindled also. Her attitude toward economic
problems was "somehow God will provide." She rarely spent
any money on herself, devoting her income to others, and
somehow she managed to work it all out. Owing to the fa-
vorable exchange rate and the low cost of living in Rapallo
she was able to live comfortably and maintain her large household on the equivalent of today's $4,000 a year.

Alice Massy-Beresford was only in her late fifties when
she moved to Rapallo, but her pale lined face, her hair which
had gone prematurely white, and her outmoded Edwardian
clothes gave her the look of a much older woman. Despite
this unremarkable exterior, she had the unmistakable allure
of a *grande dame*. Her perfect manners and bearing evoked

a more civilized and polished age. Her deep religious faith had helped her to get over disappointments in the past. Surrounded by adoring grandchildren, she found the happiness she had longed for through the years of a rather dreary marriage. In her old age these grandchildren brought her the fulfillment she needed.

While Monica was working in London or Paris, the children of course had their lessons with their governess and the two youngest attended the local school in Rapallo. Ivan had been sent to school in Switzerland. Jorgen, who elevated idleness into an art, filled his days by paying visits to neighbors and acquaintances (he was much in demand for bridge and backgammon), taking the children for walks in the afternoons after classes or swimming, and sailing with them in the summer. He also liked to supervise the work of the two villa gardeners, ordering bulbs from Holland or bringing over rare plants from the famous Villa Taranto, near Pallanza, owned by his great friend Neil McKechran. Jorgen's flower arrangements were superb; there was a far greater scope for them in Rapallo than in Denmark. Monica's room, whenever she was at the villa, was filled with tuberoses and gardenias. But Monica now had little time to enjoy the flowers. Though Rapallo represented a refuge from responsibilities, her first priority was to build up her business career. Career women, as her contemporary Coco Chanel wrote in her memoirs, were a "comparatively unknown species in the thirties."

Her first inspiration—costume jewelry—came by chance. During a visit to Venice, she made friends with the Italian glassmaker Giovanni Valdt, admiring his colorful necklaces of transparent glass beads. Some were amethyst-colored, others amber or flecked with gold. She bought some and not surprisingly they turned out to be a sensation among her friends in London and Paris. Going back to the Venetian manufacturer, she got together a large stock of necklaces, earrings made like miniature bunches of grapes, and thin glass bracelets in every shade of the rainbow which were worn by the dozen. She successfully disposed of everything. Once started, she tracked down craftsmen in Paris, ordering an ever-increasing range of models.

Costume jewelry was still in its infancy. Chanel was just starting to promote it, and Monica, through sheer chance, caught the rising tide of its popularity. She of course was her own best advertisement. "You need no other," the designer Elsa Schiaparelli told her. Business took off, and within a few months she was selling more sophisticated and expensive items, like tortoiseshell bracelets with inset gold watches, compacts, and elaborate enamel necklaces, which soon became the rage. As she had no place to display her wares, she relied on word-of-mouth promotion and personal contacts. Now and then a good friend from the Paris social world would lend a house or a flat for what was jokingly referred to as "our Monica's fashion show." One such friend was Lady Mendl, the former Elsie de Wolfe, a celebrated Paris hostess in the thirties, owner of the Villa Trianon in Versailles. At her annual party in September, she appeared wearing an assortment of Monica's bracelets and arranged for her wares to be displayed in the famous Garden Room, which overlooked the park of the Château de Versailles. Lady Mendl, who had a wonderful sense of humor, watched with "infinite amusement" her elegant women guests, dripping with diamonds and other jewels, fighting over Monica's glass trinkets, pronouncing them the *dernier cri*. The fad of course did not last, but while it did, it was of considerable help to Monica.

The move into cosmetics came by chance. Excessive use

of nail polish had made Monica's long nails brittle. At a small chemist's in Paris, just off the rue du Cirque, she found a product which she noticed "miraculously strengthened the nails." During one of her visits to England, she had it analyzed, found there was no harmful substance in it, and upon her return to Paris, finding that the chemist was retiring from business, she bought the patent for his mixture to distribute in England. She called it Nocrax. It was well advertised and soon began to show a handsome profit. Encouraged by Nocrax's success, she launched an excellent eau de cologne, Monica 55, made from an essence supplied by one of her Paris friends from the trade world of Coco Chanel. That too went well; its manufacture stopped only with the outbreak of World War II.

Monica did well as a businesswoman. Her combined profits from Nocrax, Monica 55, and costume jewelry ran to about $6,000 a year, a healthy sum sufficient in those days to pay for her children's schooling, dental expenses, travel, clothes, and incidentals. She even managed to squirrel some of it away and, advised by knowledgeable friends, invest it well. It was a considerable achievement for one whose only qualifications for business were her imagination and persistence.

The 1930s changed Monica yet again. This difficult period transformed her into an efficient businesswoman with an eye for a bargain and enough self-assurance to promote her products to strangers. She was fighting for the future well-being of her children, and her efforts were crowned with success, for she managed to give them an excellent education which enabled them to have their own successful careers. As her profit margins were small, Monica had to keep personal expenses to a minimum. In London she traveled by tube and in Paris she became an habitué of the Métro, journeying to distant suburbs to visit suppliers. Unless taken out, she ate in cheap bistros or cooked for herself on the gas ring in the garret-like room on the top floor of her friend Clara Hasselbach's apartment house in the rue de la Paix. The flat was modest and cheap, and the location conveniently central. She spent many evenings alone, writing letters to her three children: to Ivan, first at Glion in Switzerland, then at Eton; to Viggo, at his Scottish boarding school; to Varinka, who was being taught by Olga Signorini, the family governess and housekeeper.

Life was not all gloom and work. If some of her old friends did desert her, she gained others who admired her courage, originality, and style. In Paris there were dinner parties at Lady Mendl's, elegant soirées at Elsa Schiaparelli's, gourmet meals with the English couturier Edward Molyneux, and dancing evenings with friends at the fashionable nightclub Boeuf sur le Toit. In London she slipped back into her old circle of friends from the twenties: she often stayed with the painter Oswald Birley and his wife, Rhoda, a childhood friend; with her Mulholland cousins; or visited her brother Tim and his wife in their house in Wiltshire. Monica always remained faithful to the memory of her unfortunate sister-in-law Mabelle Wichfeld. In the late thirties she undertook single-handedly to look after Mabelle's son Clarence Moore, a confirmed alcoholic who for years caused her much worry and expense. Among the people she liked were two sets of couples—the Sidney Allens and the Herman Rogerses of Baltimore. They had been close to Mabelle and behaved impeccably during her last years of reverses. It was Herman and

Millicent Rogers who found themselves cast in the role of chaperons to history's most celebrated divorcée and invited Monica to meet her.

This unlikely event came about late in 1936, when Monica, like the rest of her countrymen, was stunned by the news of the crisis caused by the abdication of Edward VIII, who wanted to marry the twice-divorced Wallis Simpson. Waiting for her second divorce to become final, Mrs. Simpson was staying at Lou Vlei, a rented villa near Cannes, with the Rogers couple as her protectors and counselors. Early in 1937, on her way to Rapallo, Monica stopped off at Cannes to spend a few days with their close friends Marion and Sidney Allen. She was suffering from a bad toothache, and described the visit to her mother:

The Carlton Hotel, Cannes, March 2, 1937

Dearest Mother,

At last I am over the pain; the journey passed somehow with the help of dope but the pain was acute. . . . Marion [Allen] found me a good Swiss dentist and made an appointment for 6:30 this evening. . . .

We dined at the Villa Lou Vlei with Herman and Millicent Rogers, where Mrs. Simpson is living. I sat beside her at dinner and she came and talked with me afterwards and I played a rubber of bridge with her as her partner. Afterwards she was called to the telephone to talk to the "King," as she calls him (while the proper King and Queen are referred to as "the Yorks"). . . . I could fill several letters with the things that were said. . . . Her mailbag has now dropped to 500 letters a day but they still have to have an extra postman. The surcharge for insufficient stamping runs to over 1,500 francs a month. The ones sent to the Duke [of Windsor] in Austria are also understamped and the surcharge for them is over 3,000 francs. He refuses to accept any of them. The amusing thing is that the only letter that she ever sent him, together with some newspaper clippings, weighed too much and was sent back with the other understamped letters. She and her secretary spend every morning answering this huge correspondence; the ones they can't read are thrown away. Some letters are threatening, others rude, and others again from admirers or from the clergy (shame on them!) who disagree with the Archbishop of Canterbury and who wish to conduct the wedding ceremony. She gets gifts from all over the world; some are given to the servants in the villa, others returned. At dinner we had a sauce with the ice made from a special kind of huge walnuts that an unknown admirer had sent from India. . . . Among people who come and speak to her is an old woman who had walked 250 miles to say that "voices had told her that Mrs. S. will be murdered in a ballroom by two women." I think Mrs. S. thinks of herself as a martyred heroine. . . . She laid herself out to charm me; she admired my hair and the way it was done (the same way as hers); apparently she said to herself when she saw me: "Here is a woman who is different from others." She wanted to hear my opinion on every possible subject and insisted on discussing "the great English middle class." It was a little difficult to talk about as it was precisely the middle classes that had her thrown out of England . . . but she went on. She is common and vulgar beyond words. . . . She and the Rogerses get on each other's nerves; she wants to go out all the time, but they won't let her, and she is pretty displeased at always having to stay home, but I believe there are many people who get up and leave a restaurant when she enters, so I suppose they do not want to risk any trouble. She wanted us all to have dinner with her at the Casino tomorrow evening, but was not allowed to. It will have to be at Lou Vlei. I wonder how long the friendship will last. . . .

Increasingly Monica's life was being dominated by signs of the coming war. Loving Italy as she did and knowing the Italian character and their distaste for military adventures, she did not at first consider Fascism a danger. "What a splendidly orderly country Italy has become," she wrote to her brother Tim upon receiving a package from him in record time. She once wrote a letter of appreciation to the local Italian newspaper, *Il Mare*, after three valuable rings she had left by mistake in the lavatory on the Rome express train were returned to her by the train conductor. But Mussolini's 1935 attack on Abyssinia, followed by his growing rapprochement with Hitler, changed her view. Mussolini was now obsessed with appearing as formidable as his German counterpart. His speeches were becoming more and more extravagant. She thought he was becoming dangerously bellicose and above all anti-British, protesting against the presence of the English navy in the Mediterranean.

Monica, who since her brother Jack's death had been profoundly anti-German, had had various encounters with Nazi Germany in her travels, none of them pleasant. She had witnessed the mass hysteria of the Nazi rallies. She was appalled when Hitler reoccupied the Rhineland with hardly a voice raised in protest in England or France. Brought up without a trace of prejudice, she was repelled by Hitler's persecution of Jews. In August 1936 he staged his great propaganda coup, the Berlin Olympics. A huge, magnificent stadium had been rapidly constructed on the outskirts of the capital (only a few miles away from the already functioning but then unknown Oranienburg concentration camp). It was to be Hitler's great "Festival of Peace," before he plunged the world into war. And the world flocked to it. There were over 100,000 visitors including royalty, statesmen like Lloyd George, men of letters like Arnold Toynbee, personalities like Charles Lindbergh, all there to admire the dazzling display of radiant, blond German youth. A number of Danish leaders, including Crown Prince Frederick, were expected to attend. At one time Jorgen was tempted to join them, but Monica would not hear of it, and Jorgen remained in Rapallo.

Among those who were now being given the red-carpet treatment by Ribbentrop was the Nazi-hating Count Kurt Haugwitz-Reventlow with his twenty-four-year-old wife, Barbara Hutton, whom he married in 1935 in Nevada, a few hours after she received a divorce from her first husband, the fake Georgian prince Alexis Mdivani. Kurt's stormy marriage to the world's richest girl still had two years to run, but it was already turning out to be a heartache. The last thing Kurt wanted to do was to attend the Olympics, but Barbara, excited over the glittering party organized by the charming Italian ambassador in London, Dino Grandi, insisted on going. He went and they quarreled, another omen of a doomed alliance.

Monica had learned of Reventlow's marriage to Hutton in a dramatic telephone call from Kurt while she was in Rapallo spending the Easter holidays with her children. "There was only one telephone in the villa, and it was in a passage where everyone could hear what was said," she told her friends. "I went to answer when it rang; it was Kurt telephoning from Venice." Monica had not seen or talked to him for five years, but her husband, who remained in touch with his old friend Heini, liked to draw her attention to the glamorous life her former lover was leading. Kurt had entered the London stock market after the Crash and bought wisely. His elegant figure continued to be seen at the Paris Ritz, in

Cannes, Monte Carlo, and at Ascot after Monica had withdrawn from the scene. It was in Carlsbad, the watering place made famous by Edward VII, that Reventlow met Barbara Hutton and her father. He saw her again in Paris and soon found himself the object of romantic desire on the part of the neurotic and willful heiress. Kurt was thirty-nine; Barbara had just celebrated her twenty-third birthday. As her biographer, Jennings remarked, "After the weak and effeminate Mdivani, Reventlow's haughty, insolent looks and his obvious masculinity appealed to her." Kurt's telephone call was to inform Monica that he was "thinking of" marrying Miss Hutton unless of course Monica had at last changed her mind and would consent to marry him. With uncharacteristic patience and tenderness, he explained he had been in love with her for more than thirteen years, and he wanted to settle down and have a wife and a family of his own. "Will it be yes or no?" he asked her over the crackling line from the other side of the Alps. Monica, as she later recounted, took a deep breath. "The picture of my lonely room in Paris, the endless rides in the crowded Métro, the years and years of financial worries, all went through my mind in a flash. Of course I still loved him, and I knew him better than anyone else in the world." But her answer was again a firm no. She would not turn her back on the road she had chosen. Her family came first; her resolution had not changed since that day they had parted at Rosenlund.

In the course of their long and intimate conversation, she teased Kurt about entering the world of megamoney. She sensed that he was apprehensive and laughingly promised to remain "his good friend from afar." She then put down the receiver, mounted the stairs to her room, and closed the door.

Five

In the Shadow of War

MUSSOLINI'S heavy features were stenciled all over the town walls when Monica arrived in Rapallo to spend the summer of 1938 with her family. Since the Germans had entered Austria the previous March, there were serious rumors of war, but they were not enough to change the arcadian character of Rapallo's daily existence. Their remoteness from the world made the daily news seem unreal. On the rough shingle beach fishermen's wives sat in the sun, making elaborate lace on bolster-like pillows. Men sat barefooted, mending their nets, which they held firmly in place with their prehensile toes. Teams of mules, their bridles linked together by ropes, trudged up the steep paths carrying loads of bricks, mortar, groceries, or whatever was required by the *contadini* living on the hillsides above. The local people seemed contented. In those days, crimes or murders were unheard of in Rapallo; doors and windows were left open; there were no burglars. Foreigners were made welcome, for they supplied well-paid work. Besides the small British colony and the American expatriates, there were now Spanish refugees from the Civil

War. Most of them came from Barcelona and were well off; some Jewish refugees had arrived from Germany, hoping to move on elsewhere—but all this hardly stirred the tranquil waters.

Jorgen was busy playing backgammon at the Excelsior Casino with Princess Jane di San Faustino, an American-born Roman hostess. She was eccentric in her habits and dress—perpetual widow's weeds, white ankle-length flowing robe, and Mary Stuart headdress in black and white. She was in permanent mourning for her husband, the old prince, whom she had always professed to dislike. The children set off alone, without Jorgen, to meet their mother, who was arriving from Paris. It was a ritual strictly adhered to through the years, to await her arrival on the Paris-Rome express. "I recall the feeling of joyous anticipation," Viggo told me, "with which we used to set off for the station. Our mother was away from us more than was usual for a parent in those days. In spite of the excellent care we received from our grandmother and Olga Signorini, who loved us all, we nevertheless longed for her presence and the sense of fun and excitement she brought. I can still see the little station in Rapallo, with its orderly salvia flowerbeds and the dusty clusters of lemon and orange trees and the winding track, curving north; the Rome express would appear thundering around the bend in the corner and suddenly there she was: impeccably dressed as always—blue gabardine suit, hat adorned with a large diamond pin, long red-lacquered fingernails, as was the fashion in those days, and hands with skin so white and transparent that every vein was visible, running toward us, soft, huggable, full of laughter and love. . . . And all that luggage!"

In spite of the fact that she was constantly on the move, Monica insisted that her "hand luggage" always travel with her in her compartment. The minimum was two suitcases, a leather jewel case, a case for papers, a hatbox, a vanity case, a portable gramophone, a box of records, and a typewriter. In addition there were handbags, umbrella, cushions, traveling rug, and occasional small packages. As she was a beautiful woman and there was no shortage of porters, changing trains presented no problems. Wherever she arrived, whether it was at a hotel or a friend's house, Monica immediately opened her cases and arranged the room so that she would feel at home in it. Vases were filled with flowers, framed photos of the family were placed everywhere, and ashtrays were distributed around the room, for she was an inveterate smoker. An illusion of home was created, no matter how dismal the surroundings.

At Campo dei Fiori Monica had furnished her own room in the southwest corner of the house with attractive Piedmontese furniture, similar to French Provençal. She had the walls painted a smoky rose and decorated with eighteenth-century prints and old maps of Ireland, Denmark, and Italy. The room was pink and white, with heavy rose raw-silk curtains; a fine Turkish rug covered the parquet floor. Sunshine streamed through the two large windows facing south. It was a happy room, "one that we always entered with joy," recalled Viggo. The villa was extremely agreeable to live in. All the ceilings were high, and most of them were painted with "grisaille," *trompe l'oeil.* The rooms were cool in summer, when the shutters were drawn, and could be heated in winter by central heating and fires of fragrant olive wood in the drawing room and the bedrooms. Monica's room had a particularly attractive glazed terra-cotta fireplace. A huge terrace ran the length of the house, providing a kind of open-air living room. It was nicely secluded, full of flowers and sweet-smelling climbers, jasmine and banksia roses. Alice Massy-Beresford spent entire days in her deck chair, reading or doing crossword puzzles under a large striped umbrella. Meals were served there on the warmer winter days, for there was always sunshine on the terrace. It was a happy house. There was a strong bond of affection between the family and the servants, who remained at the villa with remarkable devotion through all the years of Alice Massy-Beresford's ownership, even during the worst years of the war.

After London and Paris, Rapallo's sun-drenched remoteness struck Monica as eerie. In London, opposition to Chamberlain's appeasement policy was growing fast; trenches were being dug in the parks. First aid was now the rage, and many of her women friends were taking a Red Cross course in the treatment of gas victims. A feeling of *déjà vu* came upon her when she happened to pass by the house in Lower Belgrave Street where she had worked in a canteen twenty-three years before, during the First World War. In France talk swirled around Daladier and Gamelin and the assumed invincibility of the Maginot Line. But at the Rapallo tennis club the talk was of the amorous exploits of the handsome bachelor Theo Rossi, the Vermouth King; of racing driver Count Trossi, who deliberately rammed his wife's car because he thought she was out with another man; and of eccentric poet Ezra Pound, tall and red-bearded, with a long jade earring in his left ear, whom Ford Madox Ford once described as playing tennis like an "inebriated kangaroo."

Back in the twenties, when Monica had visited Rapallo and first met Ezra Pound, she had genuinely admired the poet. Ezra's delight in Rapallo and the sense of liberation he felt after London and Paris, as expressed in his *Canto 17*, appealed to her. Pound described the little seaside resort as

an earthly paradise "with cliffs of amber and magic case-
ments, where bees weighted with pollen abound . . ." But she
soon came to share Yeats's opinion of Ezra as a man "who
produces the most distinguished poetry and yet in his behav-
iour is the least distinguished of men." America's great poet
was on the verge of becoming a traitor to his own country. He
had ardently embraced Fascism and hero-worshipped Mussolini, who appealed to him as an image of "tough masculinity
and a genius." Monica was both amused and horrified by
Olga's description of Ezra's return to Rapallo after an interview with Mussolini in Rome: "The town band greeted him
at the station and escorted him noisily to his lodgings on the
top floor of the Albergo Rapallo, while his wife, Dorothy, stood
on the open terrace above, cheering." Pound's popularity reflected the feelings of a wide segment of ordinary Italian people who, in spite of misgivings, felt that Fascism was the lesser
evil when compared with Stalin's Russia, Hitler's Germany,
and the impotent Western democracies. At least Italy was
quiet and people seemed to be content with the façade the
government was putting up.

Convinced that war was inevitable, Monica increasingly
concentrated on her children. British patriot though she was,
she blessed their Danish nationality, which she hoped would
keep them out of the coming conflict. There was still time,
she believed, to complete their education. Ivan, her older son,
was just nineteen, "a most promising young man," his head-
master at Eton had written. Tall, slender, with his mother's
wide-set gray eyes and his father's classical blond Nordic
features, Ivan excelled at everything he cared to turn his hand
to, from sports to bridge, at which he became a champion
player. He was intelligent and gentle and had inherited much
of his mother's charm. He was immensely popular and he

loved life. At sixteen Varinka (Inkie) was an attractive teenager with a head of blond curls, keen on sport and proficient in three languages. And there was Viggo, her youngest, sensitive, highly strung, the one who needed her most; he was going through a difficult time at Gordonstoun, a tough, rather spartan boarding school in northern Scotland, but he was adapting fast.

The children all spoke perfect English, which was the language of the house, as well as French and Italian; but with the exception of Ivan, who had spent more time than the rest of them in Denmark and was conscious that one day he would inherit Engestofte, they did not feel particularly Danish. "Denmark was my birthplace, but little else," recalled Inkie, who six years later became one of the heroines of the Danish Resistance. "We had not been able to live there since I was eight. . . . I had a grandmother and an aunt to whom I wrote a Christmas letter every year. It was a bore, for it always had to be rewritten; Daddy corrected them, as my Danish was not good enough; we always spoke English at home." Rather reluctantly, Monica sent Ivan to Berlin after Eton, to a "cultured anti-Nazi family" to learn the language. Jorgen and Monica went to visit him there. "Ivan is well and getting on perfectly," she wrote to her brother Tim, now a brigadier in the army. "We adored seeing him, but I hated the atmosphere in Berlin, charged with hysteria. It can't be very long now before the madman moves on to the next step."

To her mother she wrote from Berlin: "The only thing that made the stay at the Adlon at all bearable was Brian Taylor, who was thrilled to see us and saw to it that we were treated like royalty." Brian Taylor was a young man from a village in Wiltshire, whose ambition was to become a hotel manager. Through a chain of fortuitous circumstances, he managed to get in touch with Monica in England. Always ready to help people, she replied that she would be pleased to assist and when they met suggested that he start "at the top." In Paris she spoke to Mme César Ritz, who agreed to take on the young Englishman as a trainee. Brian duly went to Paris and did well, rising to junior manager. In 1938 he was offered a lucrative job as a member of the management at the famous Adlon Hotel in Berlin, where Monica and Jorgen saw him. She had kept in touch with her protégé and before the outbreak of war wrote suggesting he return home. Brian was eventually interned in a civilian prisoner-of-war camp in Germany. Until her own arrest in 1944, Monica kept up her correspondence with Brian, sending him food parcels and news. Her letters, now lodged in the State Archives of Copenhagen, provided many details of Monica's life during the war.

In September 1938 Chamberlain met Hitler at Berchtesgaden and promised "not to oppose" the occupation of the Sudetenland. A futile gesture, as Czechoslovakia's annexation by the Reich had already been proclaimed. A week later Chamberlain returned to Germany to meet with Hitler at Godesberg. Until the signing of the "Peace in Our Time" agreement, it looked as if war would break out at any moment.

A certain nervousness reigned at Campo dei Fiori. Tim wrote from England asking the family to see that their mother left Italy "forthwith." Unlike Monica, Jorgen, and the three children, who were all Danish citizens, it was feared that Mrs. Massy-Beresford would be interned in the event of war. Ivan, returning from Berlin that summer, described the hectic week: "Olga burst into floods of tears when she heard of Granny's imminent departure. The servants wept as if they were being beaten. . . . They listened to Mussolini's tirades on the radio, but determinedly refused to salute him with upstretched arms, as they used to, something that amused Viggo no end. Everybody helped Granny to pack. She wanted to have all her books with her, pictures and photographs, small things, big things, all her clothes and much more besides. . . . She never expected to see her beloved Italian home again. But the next morning she changed her mind and ordered that only the most necessary things be put in one or two bags. I was to accompany Granny to Aix-les-Bains, but shortly before our departure we heard Chamberlain's message about 'Peace in Our Time' and everything was unpacked and put away again."

The appeasement at Munich provided a respite from tension. It was arranged that Ivan should go to Denmark to learn the rudiments of farming and estate management on a neighbor's estate in Lolland; Inkie was dispatched to Vienna to learn German, while Monica went back to Paris to earn the family's living. She now had a new flat at rue Copernic, more spacious and comfortable than the "garret." She wrote to Viggo at Gordonstoun that she had been laid up in bed for a few days. "I have been fairly 'sickety' [sic] lately . . . am better today, which is just as well because my show is tomorrow and Thursday. Mrs. Cartwright [an American friend and client] was coming round here, but telephoned to say she did not feel well enough and would I go to her instead. So I crawled out, packed everything, and took all my stuff there; I lunched with her and sold her about 5,000 francs' worth of jewelry— also to a friend of hers, a Mrs. McEvoy, so it was all worth it. I am almost 'all square' now, so the rest will be profit. Am waiting to see a woman called Teddy Thompson, who is coming here to buy trinkets for her shop in New York." A few days later: "I went round to Lady Mendl on Sunday. She had a large tea party with all the people I had wanted to get in touch with for some time. She made them look at my things and over 4,000 francs was the result; they all want to see me again. . . . Lady Mendl insisted I send a postcard to the Duchess of Windsor *de sa part*, but I refused. I have now got where I want to in Paris and need just one more season to consolidate my finances."

Interspersed in her letters to Viggo are references to Kurt. "K is here at the Ritz. I dined with him two nights ago and we went to the cinema, the American version of *Pepe Le Moko* called *Algiers* with Charles Boyer. I read him your letter about the camera he gave you and he was very pleased." She also wrote that before Kurt went to London, "he took me to several cinemas and to the play *Le Corsaire* and sent me some lovely lilies. I went out and watched him play tennis with the 'pro' here; he plays a beautiful game; was very proud of himself and rightly so. . . . I shall see him in London."

Reventlow was back in Monica's life. The saga of Kurt and Barbara Hutton's stormy marriage had been featured in headlines in the European press. Barbara's romantic attachments and marriages were followed avidly by a public fed up with the dismal international news. "The break-up of the Reventlow marriage and the acrimonious divorce case that followed have given England its greatest sensation since King Edward VIII renounced the throne eighteen months ago for the love of Mrs. Wallis Warfield Simpson," remarked *The (London) Times*. Monica had read about the birth of Barbara and Kurt's son, Lance, and sent a note of congratulations to Kurt. But the splendors of Winfield House, their palatial home in Regents Park (now the residence of the U.S. ambassador), were a long way from her own circumstances. Then came the dramatic break-up. At one point, when a warrant had been issued for Kurt's arrest for allegedly "assaulting Barbara in their own home," Monica sent an urgent letter to his solicitor, Norman Birkett, testifying to Kurt's good character. The warrant was canceled.

That autumn, when she returned to Paris from Rapallo, she found Kurt waiting to see her. Their relationship had changed. The intensity and the passion, which had so often created difficulties between them, had gone; they were no longer young and they had led separate lives for a long time. But a deep friendship remained. She was his friend and counselor, the woman he had known longest and best. They saw each other intermittently in Paris, London, and Rapallo. Jorgen and the children welcomed him back as an old family friend. Alice Massy-Beresford, with her gentle wry humor, teased him about "Barbara's pearls" whenever she saw a necklace of fake Woolworth-like beads.

On one of his visits to London, Kurt called on Brigadier Tim Massy-Beresford. "I had not seen K for a long time," Monica's brother recalled. "It was just after Munich and the country was greatly unsettled. K arrived and declared that I was the only person with whom he could discuss things sensibly; he then asked for my views on the political and military situation, and inquired whether I would be willing to become his son Lance's guardian. . . . The reason he gave me was that he didn't wish on any account for Lance to be brought up according to Barbara's ideas. Lance was getting dreadfully spoiled as it was; he, Kurt, wanted him to grow up as an English boy, go to schools in England, etc. He produced a document for me to sign, which I did, for I had always liked K in spite of his occasional pompous airs." The document was never used.

* * *

Early in March 1939, Monica, after a successful selling
season in Paris, went to St. Moritz to meet her daughter, who
was arriving from Vienna. Kurt was there skiing, staying at
the Palace Hotel. He had just won the famous Gold Star Race
and was "wild with delight" as most of the other competitors
were thirty or under. Monica cheered him on. Later that
month she and Inkie were to meet Jorgen and Viggo in Hamburg and sail to Denmark for a brief stay. Ivan was working
on a farm in Lolland. As Monica said, "It is time for the
children to renew contact with their own country." Hitler's
march into Prague and his annexation of Czechoslovakia intervened, but after last-minute consultations they decided to
go ahead anyway.

"I expect this taking of Czechoslovakia has been a fearful
blow for many of your school friends," Monica wrote to Viggo.
"Poor souls, one has a lot to be thankful for until the day
comes when they want Denmark! . . . I am sending you a
check to cover the expenses of your travel to Hamburg. It will
be lovely to see you in less than a month now." The Easter
visit to Denmark was a success. Monica had always loved the
Scandinavian spring, which comes late. The primeval sud-
denness of roaring floods heaving under green ice floes, black
beech trees sprouting green shoots overnight, birches veiled
with yellow blossoms were exciting. At Engestofte she enjoyed
walking through the woods and the garden in an old tweed
skirt and a sweater, down gravel paths lined with snowdrops.
In the forest there were ancient beech, ash, maple, and alder
trees which in May would form a vault. In April the leaves
had not yet unfolded, but fields of wild anemones bloomed
beneath them.

They visited family, friends, and relations; they had been greatly missed in the islands. With Denmark entering an agricultural boom, perhaps the Wichfelds would be able to return to Engestofte. Friends and relations remarked that in spite of the passage of time and all her labors, Monica was still beautiful. Her looks were now enhanced by silvery streaks at the temples. Her dark hair, parted in the middle, was always in classical fashion. They spent a week with Jorgen's mother and sister in the country, stayed with the Rabens at Aalholm and with Monica's friend Suzanne Lassen, a talented painter and writer, in Copenhagen. Engestofte was still let to a local judge and his family, but the manager of the farm and the estate people were delighted to see them. Everyone wanted them to come back to the place where generations of Wichfelds had lived. Ivan's presence and his decision to remain in Denmark to study farming met with approval. The warm welcome she received strengthened Monica's tie to her adopted country; she hoped it would not be long before they were able to return to their beloved Engestofte.

Viggo's holiday from school was at an end, and Monica traveled with him as far as Hamburg. Viggo recalls that his mother was full of foreboding as they boarded the little steamer ferry at Gedser. "We stood on the quarterdeck of the ferry watching the low Danish coastline disappear, while the noise of German airplanes from the base in Warnemünde became louder and louder. Gulls circled around letting out harsh cries, and Mummy said: 'This may be the last time we shall see a free Denmark. When we come back, it will probably be an occupied country. It is possible that you will see it free again, but I doubt whether I will live to see it.' "

In July, before returning to Rapallo for the summer, Monica went over to London from Paris to see her mother. Alice

Massy-Beresford was in England for her usual round of summer visits with friends and members of the family. The outbreak of the war caught her in England and she was not to see her beloved Italian home for more than five years. In that last summer of peace, the weather was particularly radiant. Despite the general anguish among her friends, particularly those with sons or husbands about to be called up, Monica enjoyed her round of country visits. She spent an evening with her old acquaintance Lord Beaverbrook. According to Brigadier Tim Massy-Beresford, Beaverbrook, on hearing that she was returning to Italy and planned to remain there even if war should break out, suggested she "keep in touch, as occasional reports from her on the situation in Italy might be useful." Monica also saw Mrs. Churchill briefly during that fortnight. She had met the Churchills occasionally in the twenties, but she did not know them well. Now, of course, Winston Churchill represented everything she believed in.

"At this distance I cannot possibly tell you how it all came about," Tim Massy-Beresford wrote, "but I know that in 1940 our intelligence in London became aware that Monica was making useful observations on the attitude of certain types of Italians to the war, and they commissioned her to send (via America) regular reports. I seem to remember that some of them made their way to the BBC as background material for their broadcasts to Italy. You can tell from this that my sister had no intention of remaining idle through the war. This activity of hers, small as it was, may well, for all we know, have been a step which led to the job she did when she returned to Denmark and which cost her her life."

Rapallo, too, was beautiful in that last summer. "It was rather annoying the way Mummy kept talking about the possibility of war," recalled Inkie, who was back from Denmark for the summer. "It meant little to us, for we had heard so much about it in the last two years. Selfish, as all semi-grownups are, we thought, If there is a war we are all Danes and will be neutral. But Mummy kept saying, 'Don't let me forget the six o'clock BBC news. What time is it now?' It upset me when I was in the middle of some exciting story of my prowess at tennis or swimming. Daddy, thank God, never seemed to be the least interested. . . . So we swam in the Mediterranean, played tennis, ate ices, and wandered endlessly up and down the seafront with a group of Italian teenage girls, and an occasional boy turning up on an aluminum racing bike."

Returning from an early swim on September 1, Monica saw a group of people on the beach gathered around a portable radio. The Germans had crossed the Polish frontier that morning and were crushing all resistance before them. For the next two nerve-racking days, she remained glued to her radio and on Sunday, September 3, 1939, heard Neville Chamberlain announce that "a state of war now existed between Germany and the United Kingdom." Her first thought was for her brother Jack, who had given his life to defeat Germany; his sacrifice now seemed futile. She would have liked to fly back to England and offer her services to her country, but knew it was impossible. Her husband and children were Danish and neutral. During the weeks that followed, Monica felt very much isolated. Jorgen and his Scandinavian friends got on her nerves with their assertions that a European war meant prosperous times for small neutral countries. "Those unreal days, under the baking sun with the beauty of the Mediterranean around me, were among the worst I had ever spent in my life," she told her son.

After consultations with the Danish legation in Rome, it was decided that the family would remain in Italy until the situation became clearer. Viggo did not go back to Gordonstoun but continued his studies at the local school and later in Florence. A few days after the outbreak of war, Monica drove to Genoa to say goodbye to American friends who had hastily booked passage on the *Conte di Savoia*, after discovering it was the last liner sailing for the United States in the foreseeable future. While she was there, the rumor swept Genoa that Italy was about to declare war and the liner's departure was delayed for twenty-four hours. She witnessed the most dramatic scenes at the port, as hundreds of Jewish refugees and their families, suddenly realizing this might be their last chance of escaping concentration camps, fought for the privilege of sleeping anywhere, even on the floors of third-class cabins.

Once the last British and Americans had left and the *Blitzkrieg* in Poland was over, the situation in Italy began to deteriorate. Monica was warned to temper her outspoken pro-Allied comments, and new restrictions were enforced against foreigners. Only Ezra Pound remained unmolested; to Monica's fury, he went on with his exuberantly pro-Fascist broadcasts. They stopped only after Italy's surrender, when he was arrested by the American forces, taken to Washington, and put on trial.

"I was in a tram in Florence on my way to a fencing lesson," recalled Varinka. It was April 9, 1940. "I saw crowds gathered outside shops as I passed. I got off and heard the words *Danimarca* and *Norvegia*. When I got home I switched on the radio, which announced the invasion of Norway and the total capitulation of Denmark. I who had never felt Danish suddenly began to feel something, and wept with rage against

those who had stolen my country." For a short time after the
occupation of Denmark, Monica considered emigrating to the
United States with the family to join the movement for a Free
Denmark, organized by Henrik Kauffmann, the Danish ambassador in Washington. But the success of the German *Blitzkrieg* and Italy's entry into the war put an end to these plans.

Early in June 1940 loudspeakers were installed in Rapallo on the town square. Peasants streamed down from the
hills, and local Fascists, including the faithful Olga, donned
their flamboyant uniforms. Shops were closed and preparations were made for a celebration: Il Duce was to make an
announcement. Among cries of acclamation, he announced
that Italy had declared war on England and France. All communication with England was now cut off; Portugal and the
United States remained the only open channels. The Wichfelds were told by the *carabinieri*, the local police, that foreigners were no longer allowed to live in coastal areas like
Rapallo. Taking advantage of an offer from a Genoese merchant family to rent their house, Jorgen and Monica moved
to Florence, where Viggo and Varinka were studying. Viggo
had managed to rent part of a friend's villa a short distance
from the center of town. It was at the back of a quiet piazza
and spread around a colonnaded courtyard romantically
draped with wisteria.

"I fell in love with the place the moment I saw it," Monica
wrote to Brian Taylor, who was interned in Stalag XIII A, near
Nuremberg. "My sixteen-year-old son did extremely well to
find it. The old Marchesa (Elisa Imperiali) was very reluctant
to let it for a short time, but Viggo wore down all her objections. She said that she was only letting us have it 'as he was
the nicest boy she had ever met.' He went over all the inventory
with her, got a cook, ordered food and wood for the fireplaces;

when we got here he had dinner ready, fires in all the rooms, beds made, flowers everywhere and carnations in my bedroom, bought out of his pocket money. Marvelous for a boy of sixteen, don't you think?"

Florence, even in the middle of the war, was still a civilized and agreeable city to live in. The atmosphere was pro-Allied and the Wichfelds were welcomed by the local society. The children enjoyed their studies and made new friends. For Monica the highlight of her short wartime stay in Florence was undoubtedly meeting and getting to know Bernard Berenson. Her house was only a short ride from the famous villa I Tatti, where the great collector and art critic, his wife, Mary, and his lifetime companion, Nicki Mariano, lived. So far undisturbed by the war, Berenson later took refuge with friends and remained hidden from the Germans until liberation. When the Berensons had bought I Tatti at the end of the nineteenth century, it was a plain Tuscan farmhouse with fields and vineyards on the steep slopes below. They converted it into a grand Florentine villa with a formal Italian garden. At the back of the villa a forest of cypress trees covered the hillside to its summit. In spite of its proximity to Florence, it remained an idyllic place, its isolation preserved by the Arno valley and the mountains beyond.

Monica had met Berenson through an old Rapallo friend and neighbor Muriel Mavrocordato, an Englishwoman married to a Greek. Muriel took Monica and Jorgen to visit the Berensons for tea, claiming that in wartime the great man "was short of visitors and admirers." The introduction was a success; they were asked again and again, and so were their children. A friendship developed between the old aesthete and Monica, whose original mind amused and stimulated him. To Monica conversations with Berenson were like en-

tering "a new, magic world, blissfully remote from the war."
She expressed her feelings in her letters to him. Immediately
to the left after entering the house there was a square drawing
room, dominated by a beautiful painting of the Virgin by
Domenico Veneziano; on the south side of the house was a
broad terrace with a sheltered orangerie, where Berenson
spent sunny winter days reading and writing.

"Berenson was charming to us young," recalled Monica's
son. "He gave me his *Florentine Painters of the Renaissance*
and allowed me to use his marvelous library after he heard
that I was studying the history of art. I remember him as a
small, dapper man with a baldish head and a small pointed
beard. He was always beautifully turned out—wore dark city
suits in the winter and always dressed in cream or white in
the summer, with an elegant Panama hat." Whether it was
Berenson's influence or her own desire to put her unaccustomed leisure to good use, Monica read a lot during that
"glacially cold" winter in Florence. Jorgen claimed he had
never been as cold in his entire life as he was on the stone
floors of their Florentine villa.

"I have just read Hemingway's latest, *For Whom the Bell
Tolls*," she wrote Brian Taylor. "It is one of his best and now
it is finished I miss it terribly. . . . I wish I could send it to
you. . . . Am trying to get into Proust's *Du côté de chez Swann*
but have only read about 100 pages so far and am not sure
will be able to continue. It is very slow going. . . . But if you
want heavenly philosophy and humor, try to get hold of a
book of short stories, *Seven Gothic Tales* by Isak Dinesen. Her
real name is Karen Blixen, she is a Dane, and her husband
was a famous white hunter in Kenya, whom I know very well.
She lived there for years and was desperately in love with a

young Englishman, Denys Finch-Hatton, brother of Lord Winchelsea, whom I knew years ago. He was one of the first people to fly and had his own plane out there, and one day he did not come back . . . he was killed flying that plane. She left Kenya and now she is growing old with his photograph beside her; she lives in an old country place near Copenhagen. . . . I like her. She wrote another book *Out of Africa*, or some such name, but I haven't been able to get hold of it yet."

Increasingly, as the war swung in favor of the Axis, the grip of Fascism tightened. One day a close Italian friend was arrested and they heard he had been interrogated almost exclusively about Monica Wichfeld and his conversations with her. An article appeared in a Florentine paper saying that the authorities deplored that "certain Florentine families, who were expected to serve as an example to others, should associate with Danes who were outspoken and anti-Fascist." Soon after, two uniformed policemen turned up at their flat and ordered the Wichfelds to leave Florence within forty-eight hours. They returned to Rapallo, but even there the familiar *carabinieri*, who liked them, requested that they leave Italy shortly.

Monica too was becoming increasingly alienated from her Italian friends, and in some cases friendship turned into outright hostility. It was obvious by now that they should return to Denmark. The small monthly transfers of money from Denmark, on which they now greatly depended, came irregularly and often the Rome clearing house refused to cash them. "Once or twice we went and pawned a diamond bracelet of Mummy's," recalled Inkie, "in order to be able to live until the next [transfer] arrived. It was not very pleasant for Mummy, but for us it was rather thrilling. We felt we lived dangerously."

In September 1941 Jorgen de Wichfeld went to Rome to apply for exit permits which, to his surprise and relief, were issued within a few hours. The Italian authorities were delighted to get rid of the Wichfelds. The heavy trunks were packed and sent ahead, and amazingly, though they crossed a country at war and passed through cities which were being bombed, they arrived at their destination unopened and intact. Italian friends and acquaintances turned up at the station to say goodbye. Olga, who adored them all, was in tears. Monica and the children were deeply moved. Soon the Rapallo station was left behind and the train skirted the sunlit coast to Genoa, already being bombed by the Allies. After Milan and Lake Garda, Verona, Adige, and Trento came the Brenner Pass and the frontier. "We heard the stamp of boots, the metallic clatter of submachine guns, and the loud barking of commands," recalled Inkie, "as the German passport officials worked their way along the corridor toward our compartment."

Monica did not move as the door swung open. She was reading a collection of speeches by Winston Churchill; the book had a red dust jacket and Churchill's name was blazoned on it in bright yellow letters. She had promised Jorgen she would not be "unnecessarily provocative" during their journey through Germany, but found it impossible to control her animosity. While Jorgen conducted the necessary formalities in German, she continued to address her children in English. The German officials were courteous and the train moved on into Austria. They were now traveling through Hitler's realm. "It began to get dark," recalled Monica's son. "The hamper of food we brought from Rapallo was opened and its contents quickly consumed. A German officer came into our compartment and sat down opposite my mother. She glanced at him through narrowed eyes over her book and then ignored him. He was the first German in uniform whom we had seen at such close quarters. As my mother took a cigarette out of her case, he politely jumped up and held out his lighter. She lit her own and put her lighter back in her bag. Not a word was exchanged."

They arrived in Berlin the next morning. Crowds got off the train, and of course there were no porters. But Jorgen managed to get hold of an old man with a cart on which the luggage was piled, found a taxi, and they drove to the Adlon Hotel, where they could leave the luggage with the head porter, who had known Jorgen for years. As they had no ration cards, breakfast turned out to be impossible. The young people found a café where they got some *ersatz* coffee made of acorns and consumed quantities of "disgusting synthetic pink ices." They walked up Unter den Linden toward the Brandenburg Gate. The city, Monica noticed with pleasure, bore significant signs of RAF bombing raids, though it was still a long way from the devastation and the moonlike landscape to which the Flying Fortresses reduced it two years later. The triumphal avenue leading through the Tiergarten was covered over with camouflage netting, on which imitation trees had been placed. A new axis had been cut through the Tiergarten at right angles to Unter den Linden with the purpose of confusing the bombers. Monica got Viggo to memorize the new grid—he was good at drawing maps from memory—and later reported the fact to London via Sweden. A small detail, but she hoped it would be of use to the RAF.

Compared with the bustle and animation of Rome, Berlin

appeared to them extraordinarily quiet; no young people were visible in the streets. Hitler's attack on Russia was only three months old and so far the Germans were winning. Every available male had been called into the army. Troop trains for the eastern front were leaving from the Stettiner Bahnhof every few hours.

They lunched with the two Menshausen sisters, at whose home Ivan had been learning German before the war. Both violently anti-Nazi, the sisters were quite unguarded in their comments on the regime. Monica learned about the concentration camps, the genocide of the Jews, and the arrest and imprisonment of their anti-Hitler friends. As the Wichfelds boarded the train for the coastal town of Warnemünde, where ferries left for Denmark, Ada Menshausen asked Viggo to lower the window and said to him loudly in English, "When the time comes, you must try and get to England and join up. This is not a war between nations; it is a war between good and evil." Her words made a deep impression on the boy.

It was the middle of the night when the family arrived at the ferry terminal on the Baltic. A total blackout prevailed. They stood there a long time, surrounded by their mountain of luggage, until a group of sailors from a nearby warship found a cart and accompanied them into town, where a room was found above a pub in the main street. They fell asleep but were awakened almost immediately by air-raid sirens; soon bombs were exploding around them and they were dragged down to the shelter. Monica, unperturbed and fully dressed, enjoyed the firelit display while they were reluctantly forced into the shelter. There were several near-misses, and an unexploded bomb landed in the pub where they had just slept. Somehow they managed to drag all their worldly possessions out while the bomb was ominously ticking. Late the next morning they finally arrived at the harbor, where the Danish ferry was waiting. "The old captain made us welcome on board," recalled Viggo. "He remembered Mummy and Daddy from earlier journeys. Lunch was served in the warm, comfortable saloon on the upper deck. Soft Danish voices, pleasant smiling faces, crisp white linen, mountains of butter, white bread, food we had not seen for a long time. . . . Ahead of us was Denmark. We had come home."

Monica stood at the bow of the ferry in order to be the first to see Ivan. There he was, suntanned and healthy, broader in the shoulders than she remembered, waving and signaling happily. He had passed some frightful hours at Gedser, the Danish terminal of the ferry where he heard of the bombing of Warnemünde. He wondered whether he would ever see his family again. The black-uniformed German police remained discreetly in the background while Danish officials checked their passports. Monica gave them a sidelong glance. "We are not completely free," remarked Ivan as he led them to the waiting station wagon, "but at least there is no war in Denmark."

But the war had just begun for Monica.

Six

Home among Neutrals

AT THE OUTBREAK of the war, Denmark promptly declared its neutrality as it had done twenty-five years earlier. Perhaps the situation in 1914 would repeat itself and the country would be able to avoid the war's crossfire. Hitler's ruthlessness had no effect on their traditional attitude; in the spring of 1939, Denmark was the first and only Scandinavian country to sign a nonaggression pact with Germany. As Great Britain and France entered the war and German armies overran Poland, the Danes settled comfortably on the sidelines to watch the European drama unfold. In April 1940 their illusions were shattered. At 4:25 a.m. on April 9 German troops crossed the frontier between Denmark and Germany in Jutland, paratroop units were dropped at various strategic points, and a large merchant ship, carrying an assault battalion, managed to sail past the coastal forts unchallenged. With supreme arrogance, the ship moored at the Langelinie Quay in the center of Copenhagen. It was as if a liner the size of the *Queen Mary*, loaded with tanks and enemy troops, had anchored in the

Hudson River in New York or under the London Tower Bridge.

In fifteen minutes German soldiers captured the citadel, the seat of the General Staff, and proceeded to Amalienborg, the eighteenth-century royal palace. There they were met with resistance from the King's Guard; a short-lived engagement took place in the streets around the palace square. There was also an abortive defense of Vaerløse, the military airfield near Copenhagen, in which one Danish fighter plane was shot down and the rest quickly destroyed on the ground. The citizens of Copenhagen awoke to find the streets crowded with German troops and squadrons of Nazi aircraft circling overhead, dropping leaflets informing them that the capital would be bombed if any resistance was offered. The foreign minister was awakened by the German envoy early that morning and handed an ultimatum. It stated that the occupation was a "purely precautionary measure" intended to protect Denmark's neutrality while the war lasted. Denmark would become a "model protectorate." There would be no interference in the country's internal affairs; the king could remain on the throne, the Danish army and police would be allowed to carry out their duties as before. In return, the Germans would expect loyal cooperation from the Danes.

To avoid useless sacrifice, Christian X, after conferring with his ministers, ordered the troops to lay down their arms and surrender. "In this situation, which is so serious for our native land, I call upon you in town and country alike to show an absolutely correct and dignified demeanor. God keep you all and God keep Denmark." All fighting stopped. Denmark was fully occupied, within less than three hours, for five long years. Just as it needed Norway, where resistance continued throughout the war, Germany needed Denmark as a base for operations against the northern flank of the Allies, but also to ensure the continuous supply of Swedish iron, oil, and ball bearings on which their industrial machine depended. (The Norwegian port Narvik, which the Royal Navy had unsuccessfully tried to blockade at the time, was linked by rail over the mountains to neutral Sweden's iron ore mines. From there the ore made its way to Germany by way of Denmark.) An equally important consideration was the fact that Denmark represented a source of food, of which Hitler's empire was becoming woefully short. Danish food exports alone, mostly butter and beef, provided rations for over nine million Germans, nearly one-sixth of the population. It was of course much to Germany's advantage that life in Denmark should proceed as normally as possible. As the popular rhyme ran:

> Lovely Denmark, with cattle and pigs,
> All that you cherish the Germans may guzzle.
> Theirs to devour are your favorite cornrigs,
> You in return must wear a muzzle.

The occupation was a great shock to the Danish people. The country sat calm but bewildered, "like a falcon on its captor's wrist," wrote Isak Dinesen. One had to come to terms with the humiliating fact that Hitler's troops had taken the land. At first the muzzle was easy to wear. In contrast to the harsh reports coming from Poland and Norway, the average Dane found little fault with the behavior of the German soldier on his soil. The king remained on the throne, and there was a Danish government and a Danish civil service to serve as intermediary with the occupiers. What was there to worry about? In addition, the country was growing more prosperous with every month of the war. Farmers flourished, manufacturers plied their lucrative trade with the Axis powers, and Copenhagen resembled a boom town. There was little rationing; with the exception of petrol, tea, and coffee there were few shortages. With most of the Continent subjugated and German armies racing deeper into Russia, Denmark appeared to the newly arrived Wichfeld family like a land flowing with milk and honey.

Monica found the atmosphere deeply shocking. Few of their Lolland friends and neighbors welcomed the occupation. There were those like the Lassens, whose son Anders had managed to escape from the country, join the British commandos, and become a war hero. But there were also many signs of irritating smugness and they grated on Monica. "How lucky we are here in our little Denmark," said the owner of a beautiful house on the Baltic, as he ushered the Wichfelds into his dining room to a table piled with meat, fish mousses, mounds of butter, white breads, and exotic creamy desserts. Only that morning, as she listened to the BBC, Monica had learned of the new stringent rationing in England, the high morale of the people in spite of the murderous air raids, of starving but unbowed Poland, and of Norway across the North Sea putting up fierce resistance to the occupier. She wanted to be in what she called "the real world"—fighting, not meekly consuming the fruits of collaboration. She was glad that her growing children had proper food, but even this somewhat irrationally annoyed her. Dining with Kurt's brother, Heini Haugwitz-Reventlow, one evening, amid the moated splendor of his castle, she angrily remarked to one guest who extolled the virtues of being neutral, "You will discover your patriotism only when your stomach suddenly feels empty."

Sometimes she felt totally alienated. "At times I think that I don't really belong here," she wrote to her mother in England. (Her letters had to be sent a roundabout way via Sweden or through the International Red Cross.) She viewed the German presence as a personal affront and refused to go into Copenhagen, where she knew she would see Nazi uniforms and swastikas. She also intensely disapproved of Erik Scavenius, the new foreign minister. Scavenius, a realistic politician, believed that Hitler would win the war. As 1941 drew to a close, the Germans were nearing the height of their power: Hitler's writ extended from the Channel ports to the Caucasus and even further, deep into Russia. Scavenius was convinced it would be best for Denmark to reach an agreement with Hitler while there were a few cards left to play.

Resistance work in the country was barely beginning, but an early example had been set by Danish seamen. As the Germans marched in unopposed, and the free world almost contemptuously consigned Denmark to its fate, much of the royal Danish fleet of about 230 ships and 100 fishing vessels made for British ports and came under Allied control. Others sailed under the American flag even before the United States entered the war. With their well-trained crews, they helped to preserve vital supply lines and made a huge contribution to the Battle of the Atlantic. Inside the country, opposition was thinly scattered throughout the land. Sporadic actions of protest were aimed against their own government and police rather than against the occupying forces. Monica, isolated as she was in the country, found it difficult to learn what was going on. She was determined to join some kind of underground movement and knew she would not be at peace with herself unless she made a contribution to the defeat of the Nazis.

There was much to do at Engestofte and she was happy that her husband and children were back in their old home. Despite her restlessness, she acknowledged the charm of Engestofte. Driving from the ferry with Ivan, as the car turned into the home stretch and the forest gave way to rich farmland, she was thrilled to see the gray beeches reflected in the water of the lake, the pointed spire of the church, and the graceful yellow house set among the ancient trees in the park. As she stood on the garden steps, the lake seemed more beautiful than ever, with rushes swaying in the evening breeze, a flight of ducks passing over the water, a fisherman bent over the nets in his boat at sunset. She was touched by the enthusiasm and affection with which they were received on the farm by the tenants and their personnel. A gigantic feast had been prepared for them the night of their arrival; a *Welcome Home* arch was erected over the gates. Though they had not slept for forty-eight hours, they somehow managed to stay awake and sit through multiple toasts of aquavit.

Their absence of almost eleven years and the rental of Engestofte for six years to a family with five boisterous children and two dogs had left it in a parlous state. The walls had not seen a paintbrush for a decade, carpets were stained, the furniture badly in need of repair. The house was icy and little could be done about this, for it was impossible to import heaters or porcelain stoves in wartime. Jorgen had always refused to install central heating, lest it damage some of his great-grandmother Varinka's fine pieces. The only sources of heat were the wood- and coal-burning fireplaces in the rooms; logs had to be chopped and coal fetched regularly. The park had been neglected and resembled a romantic wildwood. Half the fruit trees in the orchard were dying.

Anxious though she was to seek Resistance work, Monica felt it her duty to try to transform this white elephant into a livable home. Always practical and a hoarder (she collected odd pieces of string and put them in a box labeled '*Useless*'), she had during her years abroad occasionally sent consignments of good Italian antique furniture to Engestofte, together with rolls of French linen and upholstery chintz, all of which had been stored in the vast attics, where they miraculously survived the family's prolonged absence. Further searches uncovered other prewar luxuries, like scented soap, bath salts, writing paper, and boxes of potpourri from Guerlain. Monica decided to sell some of the Victorian furniture stored in the attics, and with the proceeds (plus money held by the trustees, back income they were unable to remit to Italy) she restored the ground-floor rooms and the bedrooms. She ordered that huge piles of wood be stacked next to the church and persuaded the gardener to double as stoker. "We cleaned, patched, sewed, and wallowed in painters, carpenters, and upholsterers," Inkie recalled. "We all wore our oldest clothes all the time. . . . Mummy made lists of everything and checked the lists she had made eleven years ago. . . . Ivan came for weekends from the farm where he was studying agriculture, bringing loads of mud-bespattered clothes to wash. Exhausted from overwork, he slept till he was hauled out of bed."

By Christmas the house looked charming and fresh again, as it had when Monica first redecorated it as a bride. Jorgen impatiently awaited the spring when, with the help of a horse-drawn mower, the lawns near the house would be cleared and he could again indulge his passion for flowers by planting hundreds of tulips and cowslips. At the end of the first week of December, while they were staying with the Sigfried Rabens in their lavish, well-heated house in the country, news came of the Japanese attack on Pearl Harbor and Roosevelt's declaration of war. "Of course the Japanese will be beaten in no time, as all their houses are made of paper," a neighbor observed. Monica smiled at such naïveté, but she knew the tide had begun to turn. She wondered about her brother Tim, who had been ordered to Singapore. (Tim was taken prisoner by the Japanese.) Every night she rushed to her room to hear the late-evening BBC news broadcast.

The shortage of petrol was felt most acutely in the countryside. At Engestofte the local bus service, which stopped at the gates to the park and provided a link with Maribo, was canceled. Bicycles and horse-drawn carriages became regular means of transport. In some ways life returned to what it had been in Jorgen's grandfather's day: distances suddenly seemed enormous and traveling was not to be undertaken lightly. Monica's early training in Ireland proved useful. She knew how to handle horses, was adept at carriage driving, and whenever they had to visit or go shopping, it was she who took the reins. Viggo, who was nearing eighteen and dreamed of escaping to England to join up, recalled: "Mummy dressed in her lynx-lined coat and spiky fur hat, handling the horses like an expert. Wrapped in our fur-lined rugs at the back, we sat singing at the top of our voices, while the carriage sped through the woods white with hoar frost."

That winter Jorgen and Monica celebrated a delayed silver-wedding anniversary (they had been married in June 1916). Neighbors and friends came from all over the countryside in pony traps, charabancs, and polished antique carriages, which looked as if they had been borrowed from museums. Monica, wearing Mabelle Wichfeld's tea gown from the twenties, presided at the end of a long dining-room table, covered with a damask cloth woven on the estate in earlier times. There was tea from Great-grandmother Varinka's silver Russian samovar, chocolate, and assorted sandwiches and cakes. Afterward there were card games for the older generation and dancing to the gramophone for Ivan and Inkie's friends.

The anniversary was a significant occasion for Monica. "We had our silver wedding anniversary last week. In fact, it was 25 and a half," Monica wrote to Brian Taylor at his prisoner-of-war camp. "It was a bit of a milestone in my life. How one changes . . ." The spirited young Irish girl, married to a sophisticated Danish diplomat ten years older, had indeed succeeded in preserving her often tempestuous marriage. There was now an unbreakable link of friendship between Monica and her husband, mutual devotion and commitment, tinged perhaps with some resignation on her part. Jorgen on his part worshipped her. Since their return to Denmark he had made an effort to take on the role of head of the family. Monica was no longer the breadwinner on whose shoulders everything rested. It was Jorgen, with his increased income from the farm, who now controlled the family finances.

And Kurt? In July 1940, when the Wichfelds were still in Rapallo, he sailed for the United States, ostensibly to be with his son Lance. During their farewell telephone conversation, Monica had begged him to join the Free Denmark movement in Washington led by the Danish ambassador, Henrik Kauffmann. Instead, Kurt went to Sun Valley, and later to California, where he joined the set of European expatriates and draft dodgers. Disappointed, Monica removed his photograph from her night table, where it had stood for twenty years. In July 1942 Kurt married Margaret Astor-Drayton, an attractive and rich American woman. His letter took a long time to reach Denmark, and by then Monica was deeply involved in underground work.

Kurt's departure from her life did not affect her friendship with his brother, Heini. They had known each other for a long time and she enjoyed Heini's cultured taste and wry wit. Heini took particular pleasure in seeing Monica and regaling her with juicy details of Barbara Hutton's absurd behavior at Hardenberg as Kurt's bride. He was genuinely delighted to have the Wichfelds back at Engestofte. But now she had to talk to him about a serious matter. Heini had made a great mistake. Together with a group of landowners whose sympathies were pro-German, he had signed the "Declaration of Goodwill to the Occupier," which the Danish Agricultural Ministry had drafted, presumably to justify the vast quantities of farm produce exported to Germany from large estates like Hardenberg. Heini was not pro-German, but in his languid way he was all for the "easy life" and let himself be persuaded to put his name to the paper. Monica heard about it and was determined to make him withdraw his signature. "It is unthinkable," she announced in her straightforward manner, "that a friend of mine should be associated with a declaration of goodwill to the occupier." Difficult as it was to move about during that autumn, she decided to go to see him.

She harnessed two bay horses to a small high-wheel carriage that Grandmother Varinka had used for her calls in the neighborhood and set off along the sandy, beech-lined road to Hardenberg. The road hugged a vast deer park and forest, then turned into a broad chestnut avenue whose sandy surface was raked daily in a herringbone pattern. The avenue led to a stone bridge, approached through tall yew hedges, and suddenly the castle appeared—a tall, square, weatherbeaten building with four round towers topped with bulbous copper spires. It stood on a green expanse of lawn, falling steeply to the moat which surrounded it on all sides. Beyond were two lakes, one with a red-and-gold Chinese pavilion floating on a minuscule island of its own. As she drove under the arch into the castle courtyard, a footman in full livery ran to take over the reins and lead the horses to the stable. Harald, the black-clad butler, greeted her with a welcoming smile and led her up the thickly carpeted stairs, past tapestries and family portraits, to the corner drawing room.

A tall redheaded man with a shy smile affectionately embraced her. He had guessed the purpose of her visit, but allowed her to be the first to broach the subject. Heini was well aware that his way of life was doomed in the postwar world. Unlike his brother, he was well versed in European history and was even something of an expert on the reign of Augustus the Strong of Saxony. Despite his feigned detachment, he carefully followed current events, even managing to obtain the daily Swiss papers from secret sources in Copenhagen. At lunch he diverted the conversation to "the good times they all had in the thirties" at the Danieli in Venice or on the Riviera. Monica let him get away with it over lunch, but as they strolled in the park, she turned and asked him bluntly to withdraw "that signature." History does not record their exact conversation, but Heini journeyed to Copenhagen two days later and made the necessary arrangements. After the war, when the inevitable reaction against collaborators began, Heini Haugwitz-Reventlow had every reason to be grateful to Monica for what she did.

*   *   *

The winter of 1941–42 was the coldest since 1871. The lake in front of the house was frozen solid and lorries drove over its surface to the islands to fell timber. Fishing through the ice, a traditional occupation, was harder than ever because of the extraordinary thickness of the ice. As the house was getting unbearably cold, Monica and Jorgen decided to move to Copenhagen in January for two months. This would enable young Viggo to continue with his architectural studies and give Inkie a chance to see her contemporaries and meet young men. Many of the neighboring families on Lolland had moved to town that winter to avoid heating their houses. In spite of the blackout and the occupation, the capital had never been livelier. Monica was also hoping to establish contact with one of the underground cells which she felt must by now exist in the capital.

Just before Christmas came a charming letter from Bernard Berenson, written at I Tatti in Florence, wishing her a good year to come and complaining about the "icy cold" in his villa. He sent words of encouragement to Viggo, urging him to continue with his architectural studies. "I was so delighted to get your letter," Monica replied, "and to hear that in spite of the cold you are well and enjoying life in your lovely villa." She guardedly went on to describe life in wartime Denmark and told him about her son's engagement to Hanne Basse, whose parents Berenson had known in Rome. She asked for news of mutual acquaintances in Florence and ended by sending him, his wife, Mary, and Nicki Mariano the family's warmest New Year wishes.

Pension Berg, where they stayed in Copenhagen, was comfortable and beautifully heated:

Here I am in Paradise, perched up in a sort of eagle's nest on the top floor, peering out at the icicles through a haze of central heating and cigarette smoke [Monica wrote to Brian Taylor]. And what a comfortable existence! I only need to press a button and minions appear to fulfill my slightest whim; and they are not wearing rubber boots over bare legs, as our Birgit does at Engestofte. . . . No mice, moths, or owls, no fear of thieves breaking in, as they do these days in the country; instead I am surrounded by tinted walls, shaded lights, pale blue linen, flower vases filled with palm sprouts! . . . I am materially happy for the next two months; as for the spiritual side, well, that is something else again, but we will talk of it some other time. [She goes on to describe the unprecedented cold.] I wake up to the sound of shovels scraping the streets outside; the snow is piled in humps six feet high along the sidewalks and so far the authorities have not caught up with carting it away. The house opposite has a lovely lacework of icicles three or four feet long, stretching the length of the block. . . . For several days this week we couldn't see out of the windows, which were frozen, and lived in a sort of aquarium out of which grew strange contorted plants and ferns made of crystal. . . . The weather is conducive to reading. I have had an orgy of [Louis] Bromfield, just lately a book of short stories, *It Takes All Kinds*, and *Night in Bombay*. I have come to the conclusion that he is not a really good writer, but perfect to pass the time in a train. . . . I am also running through a light book of John Steinbeck's, *Tortilla Flat*, very amusing and rather like Erskine Caldwell's *Tobacco Road*; otherwise am busy mending and getting the children's social life organized.

In that second winter of the German occupation—the coldest Scandinavia had experienced for a century—the streets of Copenhagen were unusually silent; there was hardly any traffic. The canals in the heart of the old city were frozen solid. On nearby Gammelstrand one could see the fishwives, in their traditional red-and-black clothing, skinning cod and sole with their bare hands. The lakes which ring the old town had become improvised rinks where brightly clad young people skated to music. The swans, ducks, and seabirds suffered, swimming endlessly in the few remaining open pools near the shore. This troubled Jorgen, who collected baskets of dried bread from the Pension Berg kitchen and, accompanied by Inkie, went down to the lake before lunch to feed the birds.

Few German soldiers were visible in town, apart from those at the port and the sentries outside the hotels requisitioned by the General Staff. There was as yet no obvious Gestapo headquarters in the Town Hall Square (Dagmar House was requisitioned later that year). Strøget, the city's fashionable street, which runs through the center of old Copenhagen, was lined with luxury shops. The big department stores like Illum and Magasin-du-Nord were crowded with shoppers and even held fashion shows. Bookshops still displayed novels in English by Charles Morgan, Hemingway, and Steinbeck. The Royal Theater held nightly performances of the ballet, opera, and plays; the smaller theaters and the circus were crowded every night, and cinemas still showed good prewar English and American films. In spite of the nightly blackout, restaurants were always full; those with dance floors, like the Adlon, were open virtually all night with cabaret acts imported from Paris, Vienna, and Stockholm. The war created a new class of rich—the wholesalers whose warehouses were full of prewar goods that now commanded many times the original cost, the manufacturers who traded with Germany at great profit, and the farmers whose products fetched high prices. They all spent money freely while the good times lasted.

From across the frozen Baltic one could almost hear the Germans machine-gunning the Polish Resistance, and the clanging of the iron gates of the newly constructed Warsaw Ghetto, into which thousands of Jews were being herded. There was an overwhelming feeling of geographical isolation that winter and Monica was not the only one who felt it. Denmark was cut off both politically and physically. The ground was frozen as far as the Swedish coast. Ships lay embedded in ice in the harbor, their rigging encrusted with icicles. All possible escape routes were unoperational and would remain so until the arrival of spring thaws. People felt they were living in a time capsule.

There was passive resistance in the form of a tremendous revival of the national spirit. Danish flags and pennants fluttered from every building, Danish men wore the king's enamel badge with his cipher and crown in their buttonholes. Students donned their red-and-white Danish caps. Every morning hundreds of people gathered in the square in front of the Amalienborg Palace to cheer the king as he was about to start on his daily ride. Christian X played a vital part in strengthening his country's morale. Each day he left the palace at eleven o'clock to ride through the streets. Bolt upright in the saddle, blue eyes gazing firmly ahead, he never acknowledged the salutes of the German soldiers who sprang to attention as he passed. The often-repeated story has it that one puzzled German trooper asked a boy, "Who is the old gentleman who rides past here every day?" "He is our king." "If he is the king, where is his bodyguard?" The boy answered proudly, "*We* are his bodyguard."

* * *

(Above, top) The de Wichfeld estate and house, Engestofte, in Maribo, Denmark. (Below) Pencil drawings of Jorgen and Monica de Wichfeld in the 1930s.

(Opposite, top to bottom) Monica and her three children: Ivan, Varinka, and Viggo in a sled at the doorway of Engestofte; in a handcart during a summer at Rapallo; and the boys "smoking" with their mother. (Above) Monica at far left with Danish neighbors on her estate. Kurt Reventlow is second from left. (Below) Monica and Kurt in Monte Carlo with the latter's limousine.

(Opposite, top) Monica and Jorgen (at right) with the Sidney Allens (at left) and an unidentified companion, at a Paris restaurant. (Bottom) Monica (at right) with tennis champion Suzanne Lenglen and the Grand Duke Dmitri of Russia.

Kurt Haugwitz-Reventlow

Monica de Wichfeld

(Opposite, top) Monica and her sons in Copenhagen in 1943, at the time of Ivan's wedding. (Bottom) Jorgen with his dogs, Kim and Domino. (Left) Wartime photos of Monica's daughter, Varinka, and her husband, Flemming Muus, a leading figure in the Danish Resistance.

One of the last photos of Monica and Jorgen, taken during the war.

Inkie and Viggo, together with their young Danish friends, joined in a campaign of baiting the enemy. They would get off a bus the moment a German soldier boarded it; demanded their bill in a restaurant if a group of Germans walked in; sported the round knitted blue-and-white cap, in the colors of the RAF, which made its appearance that winter. Viggo wore a Union Jack in his buttonhole for a month, but was caught outside a cinema and fined five kroner by a Danish judge. Inkie recalled that, in a cinema, "Viggo clapped when the Union Jack was hoisted in a film about the evacuation of Dunkirk. I followed suit with fear in my heart. The entire audience began to clap. We had started a demonstration. . . . The lights went on and a harassed manager came out demanding that the ones who started stand up. We sat very still. After five minutes the lights went out and the film continued. We heaved a sigh of relief."

Hoping to cajole the Danish press into submission, the Germans initially avoided direct censorship. At first the Danes were satisfied to read the watered-down version of events in the supervised press, but at the beginning of the second year of occupation many illegal leaflets and secret newspapers with up-to-the-minute war news, complete with maps and photographs, began to appear. From one of them Monica learned details of an event that had been puzzling her. Just before they moved to Copenhagen, the press had reported that two parachutes had been found in the neighborhood of Haslev, a town about fifty miles away. She now learned from one underground paper, passed on to her secretly by a friend, that the parachutes had belonged to Mogens Hammer and Carl Bruhn, a Danish doctor, both of whom were sent from London to build up the Resistance network. Unfortunately Bruhn's parachute failed to open and he was killed. Hammer survived and he was successfully spirited back via Sweden. Monica was immensely cheered by the news. Obviously *something* was happening.

Though from the very beginning a steady flow of military intelligence was forwarded to London via Sweden by a group of Danish officers, British encouragement of the Danish underground was slow in starting. The so-called Strategic Operations Executive (SOE), created by Winston Churchill, was reluctant to divert resources to a neutral country at a time when so many other places needed help and advice. After the failure of Dr. Bruhn's mission, another attempt to send London-trained Danish advisers occurred in April 1942, but it too ended in failure because of lack of support in Denmark. Everyone listened to the BBC broadcasts, and generally people were sympathetic to the Allies, but beyond that they were reluctant to commit themselves. "You must remember," British advisers were told, "we have our own government and our king is continuing in office. We are not Norway." The Danish police, "more deadly than the Germans," worked in close collaboration with the occupier and were universally feared. Nor did Denmark's geography, its flatness and lack of places to hide, lend itself to covert operations. It was not until March 1943 that real sabotage and organized resistance began. Soon after this Monica was put in charge of underground activities in her province.

Of course she had involved herself with the network long before that. Her first direct contact came through the Communist writer Hilmar Wulff. A short distance from the main house at Engestofte, between the woods and the lake, was a half-timbered cottage, called Skovbyhus, which belonged to the Wichfeld estate. It had stood empty for years, and when

Monica decided it should be put to use, she advertised it for rent. A person she had never heard of, Hilmar Wulff, replied that he and his family wanted to share it with a well-known Danish poet, Halfdan Rasmussen. Soon after returning from Copenhagen, Monica decided to call on the new tenants. Peeping cautiously through a window, she and Inkie saw a woman frying a chicken on a shovel over the cottage stove. Monica knocked on the door, which opened after a long pause. A small man with large horn-rimmed glasses introduced himself as Hilmar Wulff. He offered them cigars; cigarettes were hard to get. It was obvious that their host was totally indifferent to his surroundings. The room was full of empty beer bottles, and was strewn with newspapers and rows and rows of books on the floor. The furniture consisted of a sofa-bed, a few half-broken chairs, and two good modern pictures on the wall. Monica stayed for an hour discussing recent books and art, gradually feeling her way into politics. She called again a few days later and this time, as she was leaving the cottage, she asked boldly, "Do you read *Free Denmark?*" (*Frit Danmark* was one of the Resistance papers.) Wulff answered, "Yes, would you like to borrow copies?" Contact had been established; Hilmar Wulff became one of Monica's closest collaborators on Lolland.

Hilmar Wulff has his own recollection: "When I moved to a cottage on the Engestofte estate, there was as yet no real collaboration between the various scattered units, many of them Communist, as we were the first in the field. I quickly established contact with comrades in Maribo, who worked well and reliably with illegal newspapers but lacked funds. Before I met the Wichfelds I made discreet inquiries about their attitude toward the Germans, for it was not unusual for landowning families to be pro-Nazi. But I was quickly reassured on this point. The lady of the manor was English by birth and the entire family were openly pro-British. . . . After two or three meetings Mrs. Wichfeld gave me to understand that she wanted to take part in underground activities. At that time I was concerned with establishing a distribution network for *Free Denmark* and *Country and People* [*Land og Folk* was the official paper of the Danish Communist Party], which in fact was being duplicated in the cottage. We were badly in need of money and I suggested that she begin by collecting funds for the underground press."

It is not surprising that Hilmar Wulff found it hard to collect funds for his underground paper, for Denmark had always feared Russia, the giant too geographically close for comfort. Hitler's attack on Russia was greeted with satisfaction, the Communist Party was outlawed, and diplomatic relations with Moscow were severed. Under pressure from Ribbentrop, Foreign Minister Scavenius signed the Anti-Comintern Pact and the government agreed to the formation of a Free Danish Corps to fight alongside the Germans in the East. The corps turned out to be a fiasco, disliked by the German army and hated at home. As the war dragged on, public opinion in Denmark was becoming increasingly influenced by German propaganda presenting Communism as the principal danger to the world and calling for "a crusade against Bolshevism." Nevertheless, as in France, it was the Communists who produced the first underground newspapers in Denmark and encouraged others to follow.

The fact that Wulff was a self-confessed Communist did not bother Monica in the slightest. What mattered to her was that he was fighting the Germans; she would have made common cause with the devil if it meant help in defeating the Nazis. She deployed her considerable powers of persuasion on her friends, neighbors, and acquaintances, and collected donations to "a good cause" from everybody she dared ask. On her next visit to the cottage, she handed Wulff an envelope containing several hundred kroner; this was followed by further handsome amounts. During 1942 their collaboration expanded and more and more underground publications appeared.

They were an incongruous pair of associates—the handsome, elegant lady of the manor and the squat left-wing intellectual who wanted to bring down the established order after the war. "Mrs. Wichfeld could not help but know that the money she collected and gave from her own purse was going to a working-class party, which certainly did not have the welfare of the landed estates on its program. On the contrary, we firmly intended to abolish them," Wulff recalled. "But from the very first she placed the fight for Denmark's freedom above politics. . . . With her penetrating intelligence and worldly wisdom, she combined a freedom of spirit so broad and so extensive that it transcended all social considerations." Monica's son Viggo recalled how one day he was looking for his mother and found her upstairs in her bathroom. "She was washing out her stockings in the basin, under the old-fashioned polished brass taps. Hilmar Wulff, the Communist writer and journalist, was perched on the wooden lavatory seat. They were discussing Proust. . . ." Walking in the park at Engestofte, they talked about Steinbeck's *Grapes of Wrath*, a book Monica was then reading. Wulff failed to convince her of Karl Marx's virtues, but no amount of disagreement could affect their collaboration. As Monica said, "After the war we can once again quarrel about our political beliefs, but just now we must concentrate on immediate problems."

Monica joined the Resistance movement on three levels within the space of months. Hilmar Wulff was apparently her first contact. Erik Kiersgaard, a young insurance salesman and cousin of the Engestofte tenant farmer, was next. Tall, broad-shouldered, and silent, with the blond outdoor looks of a Viking, he was at the house one day, ostensibly to assess the estate, and Monica asked him to lunch. With her keen intuition she soon realized that he was "involved" and trustworthy. After lunch, as they toured the house, she explained that she was "in it." Kiersgaard had already suspected this. He himself was forming a sabotage unit on Falster, and was looking for places to store arms and explosives. Could she help? "Yes," she replied. Her third contact, at the highest international level of the underground organization, was made through Bobby Moltke, one of the most attractive figures on the political scene. Thirty-six years old, rich, handsome, and a bachelor, he was the son of an American mother (Nina van Rensselaer Thayer of Boston) and of Denmark's former Minister of Foreign Affairs.

Count Carl-Adam Moltke, nicknamed Bobby, had been busy trying to bolster his country's will to resist from the early days of the German occupation. Bobby Moltke had extensive contacts in the United States and Europe. It was he who, together with a handful of men of his age, had helped to set up a Danish intelligence unit in Sweden to channel information to England via the British legation in Stockholm. A Danish newspaperman, Ebbe Munck, went to Sweden as correspondent of the Copenhagen *Berlingske Tidende* and remained there through the war. He worked in close contact with Ronald Turnbull, sent from London to Stockholm in February 1941 to organize and control SOE activities in Denmark, under the cover of press attaché to the British legation.

Bobby Moltke frequently traveled as a courier between Copenhagen and Stockholm. One of his most daring exploits was to help organize the spiriting away to London of the famous Danish nuclear physicist, Niels Bohr. This operation was to have a crucial effect upon the course of the war.* For a long time Bobby Moltke managed to evade arrest, but early in 1944 he was "compromised" and had to escape via Sweden.

In the spring of 1942 Bobby Moltke was still acting as the jolly man-about-town, editor of a humor magazine in Copenhagen, part of the young social set to which both Inkie and young Viggo belonged. Monica had of course met Bobby a number of times, but being of a different generation had little direct contact with him. Their meeting took place by coincidence through her son Viggo.

In the summer of 1942 Viggo, then eighteen and a half, decided to escape to England via Sweden and join up. He telephoned his mother from Copenhagen one afternoon and in cautious language gave her to understand that he was leaving the next morning to travel "to our homeland." She immediately packed a suitcase and, using the last drop of her precious petrol to get to the station, caught the evening train to Copenhagen. She learned that Viggo had got a job as deckhand on a schooner leaving early the next morning for the island of Bornholm and a succession of Swedish ports. He jumped ship the moment he reached Sweden, but unfortunately he was picked up by the Swedish police. At pains to preserve Sweden's neutrality, they were constantly on the lookout for young Danish men. He was led to his ship under escort and sailed with it back to Copenhagen. Monica's re-

---

*Niels Bohr brought back vital information about the construction of the V-1 and V-2 rockets and of German work on the atomic bomb.

action was a natural mixture of pride and relief. That weekend, instead of returning to Engestofte, they went to visit
Countess Moltke at her fine rococo-style country house,
Christiansholm. Viggo was staying on, but Monica decided
to catch the Sunday-evening train to Copenhagen and Bobby
Moltke accompanied her to the local station. As he subse-
quently told Viggo: "As we walked down the long, dark lime
avenue to Klampenborg, your mother suddenly took me by
the arm and swung me around, so that we faced each other.
She told me that she had reason to believe that I was closely
connected with the Resistance and she wanted to be of use
in the most active way. She was extremely persuasive and I
promised to arrange it for her." Moltke was the crucial contact
who introduced Monica to the inner core of the organization.
Through him she was asked to arrange "reception commit-
tees" for arms drops in her province; Engestofte was desig-
nated as *the* safe house for fugitive parachutists. Monica took
on this assignment with full knowledge where it might eventually lead her. It led directly to arrest and her death sentence.

That spring and early summer Monica concentrated her
efforts on raising money for the distribution of the Resistance
papers in her province. There was dismal news from the fighting fronts. Hitler's armies under Rommel drove into Egypt,
threatening the Suez Canal and the supply lines into India.
Cairo, the hub of communications, was in danger of falling
into Rommel's hands. Following the disaster of Pearl Harbor,
Singapore fell to the Japanese on February 15, 1942. The
British commander surrendered with 70,000 of his men,
among whom was Monica's brother Tim, Brigadier Massy-
Beresford. He was taken prisoner and sent to a camp in For-
mosa and Monica did not live to see him again. The fall of

Singapore was a great disaster and Hitler's propagandists re-joiced. It was not until the Battle of Stalingrad in November that the tide of Axis victories slowly began to recede.

In spite of Allied reverses, the secret newspapers in Denmark multiplied. Hilmar Wulff's *Land og Folk* now came out in twenty-one Danish cities and in five different sections of Copenhagen. Its production was so perfectly concealed that it continued publishing all through the war.

In the early summer the *Students' Information Service* made its appearance. Run by a student group, most of its members in their early twenties, it soon reached a national circulation of over 20,000 copies. Once it was even printed on the lower floor of the Gestapo Headquarters, while Nazi typewriters clattered upstairs. By the end of 1942, there were forty-eight secret newspapers with a combined circulation of 300,000 copies; in the late stages of the war, there were 166 of them with a circulation of two and a half million. Because of its lively style, *Free Denmark* was the most influential. Its two leading spirits were the chairman of the Communist Party, Axel Larsen, and the former Conservative minister John Christmas Møller; its editorial committee represented all shades of political opinion from the right to the extreme left. Axel Larsen was arrested in the autumn by the Danish police and handed over to the Gestapo; he spent the rest of the war in a concentration camp.

News flowed from the BBC, from Swedish sources, and from the Danish press service in Stockholm, created by Ebbe Munck. For geographical reasons, radio communication between Denmark and the free world was better than in Norway or any other occupied country. Morale was boosted further by the calm voice of the BBC; its bulletins, which the Germans never managed to suppress, were received clearly. Since most

Danes had a basic knowledge of English, they were regularly listened to, even in the more remote parts of the country. Monica's activities were geared to the BBC's regular timetable of broadcasts.

Along with the underground press, sabotage was also on the increase. Many people who wished for something more than passive resistance shrank from the idea of sabotage because of the consequences to innocent civilians, but in the summer of 1942 a group of schoolboys burst on the national scene, putting their elders to shame. They called themselves the Churchill Club. Together with other young people in Ålborg, a small town in Jutland, they formed a sabotage group which carried on the destruction of German weapons and ammunition, and managed to burn vehicles and railway cars assigned to troops going to suppress resistance in Norway. They were responsible for at least twenty-five acts of sabotage; their courage, humor, and daring earned them popularity at home and admiration abroad. (The group's exploits even inspired an American cartoon-strip series.) The net eventually closed on them, but three young men kept up their private war in nocturnal expeditions from the local jail. With a smuggled hacksaw they sawed through one of the bars of their cell, so it could be removed and replaced at will. They did nocturnal damage to German cars, and grounded planes until one night, during an air raid, they were caught by the Danish police. The Germans were furious, there was a lengthy court trial and they all ended up in jail until the end of the war. The public relished reports of their escapades, their conduct in court, and their repeated explanation: "When older people won't do anything, we have to!"

A further wave of organized sabotage swept the country in the course of the summer. Special groups, recruited by the

Communists from former volunteers in the Spanish Civil War, managed to infiltrate into Denmark via Finland. Hilmar Wulff made common cause with Erik Kiersgaard. Monica, who was now helped by Inkie, worked in the background.

"Erik now came more often," recalled Inkie. "Once, on unpacking his things in the guest room, we found his sole luggage consisted of a pistol and a pair of socks, the former inside the latter. He evidently was not used to houses where the maids unpacked; luckily for him we had no maids at the time. . . . Another day while visiting Hilmar, I was asked to urgently procure some hair dye. Apparently 'a friend' had got into trouble for burning some stores stacked in a railway yard on their way to Germany. He needed a 'change of air'— Sweden maybe? I bicycled to Maribo and bought a bottle of hair dye. I never saw the result, but was told it was very successful. Later that month Erik rang from Copenhagen: Could he bring a friend for a fortnight or so? Mummy answered the telephone and said, 'Yes, of course.' He would be Viggo's new tutor, coming for an interview. 'If he turns out well, he can stay longer.' (This for unwanted ears that might have been listening in. Daddy was told the same story, just on the principle that what you don't know you can't tell.) Erik arrived in the evening; the 'friend' was a bit obviously dyed, but a nice young man. I only saw him that day, as I had to go off to one of the usual weekend parties. Appearances had to be kept up. But during our conversation I noticed that our 'tutor' was exceedingly nervous. At one point he broke down and told me that many of his friends had been arrested and one had been shot. I could see that he needed a rest, as it was unwise of him to confide in me. He did go off to Sweden before I got back from my weekend. I never saw him again, so I expect he made it."

Monica did everything to ensure that, apart from her daughter, her family was not involved in her clandestine work. Jorgen, busy with his garden, plants, and trees, and not particularly interested in the war, remained blissfully unaware of what was going on around him. Ivan was away most of the time, farming. Viggo, the one closest to his mother's heart, was drawn into the secret at the very last; she thought him too young and vulnerable to confide in. But her daughter, Varinka, was another matter. From an early age Inkie had always stressed her Danishness, in unconscious opposition to her mother, who hoped her children would turn out totally English. There is no doubt that Monica deliberately gave birth to both her sons in England to give them the right to British nationality. By sending them to schools in England she did her best to turn them into Englishmen. Jorgen never expressed opposition or suggested schools in Denmark even for Ivan, his elder son and heir. As it turned out, Ivan remained convincingly Danish, devoted to his father and to Engestofte. Despite outward appearances of a peace-loving nature, he had as strong a will as his mother, whom he adored but with whom he did not always agree. Like his father, he was not interested in politics; farming consumed all his attention.

In Italy, as a teenager, Varinka had been much influenced by their governess Olga's views and had many friends among the extreme right-wing refugees from Barcelona. She then adopted a strictly neutral attitude to the war, probably out of contrariness to her mother, whose "obsessive patriotism" sometimes annoyed her. As a result, Monica had only her young son Viggo to share her anguish at France's defeat or her joy after Churchill's inspired speeches. But Inkie's attitude changed when Germany occupied Denmark, just as Monica's obsession subsided when it found an outlet in action. Working for the Resistance brought mother and daughter close together.

Sabotage, though still unprofessional and causing negligible damage, was steadily increasing. It was a weapon directed at the government, warning it against its policy of accommodation. Foreign Minister Scavenius had to walk a tightrope between the growing resentment in his country and the German threat of reprisals. Hitler was taking a personal interest in Danish problems and voiced his irritation with *"diesem lächerlichen Ländchen"* ("this ridiculous little country"). German soldiers loved to be posted there; they called it "the whipped-cream front." Hitler now decided that the Resistance *had* to be crushed. If the government was unable to do it, the Germans would step in. The situation was suddenly aggravated by the tragicomical "telegram crisis." Every year since the occupation Hitler had sent the Danish sovereign a long telegram of good wishes, conveyed to the palace on King Christian's birthday by the German minister. Each year the king replied with a curt "Best thanks." This abrupt tone had already been noted with dissatisfaction by Ribbentrop, but he did not deem it important enough to bother the Führer. This year on September 26 the annual telegram, more fulsome than ever, was delivered to the Sorgenfri Palace, where King Christian and Queen Alexandrine were in residence with their little granddaughter Princess Margrethe, now the queen. The king replied with a short "Thank you." Hitler happened to be in Berlin and in a bad mood when the reply came. He flew into a towering rage. The reply, he announced, was an insult, and he fired off an instant reply: "The Danish king has answered my telegram in the way in which one accepts a consignment of goods. The king must realize that in present circumstances a telegram from the Führer is a singular honor and that an answer such as His Majesty has given is an insult to the Führer and to the whole German Reich. The great Führer will know how to prevent the repetition of such an episode in the future. Accordingly, the German minister in Copenhagen will immediately be recalled and the Danish minister in Berlin sent home forthwith."

When Hitler's telegram reached the palace, one of the courtiers noted that the queen "spent several mornings telephoning friends in various parts of the country to inform them of Hitler's outburst. The royal family expect to be arrested on account of Hitler's fury." Svend Truelsen, a member of a pro-Allies military group, reported to his opposite number in Stockholm: "The political front has been ominously quiet since the 'telegram crisis.' Neither Mr. Mohr [the Danish minister in Berlin] nor Mr. von Renth [the German minister in Copenhagen] has returned to his post. There is a crisis, but the Foreign Office does not quite know how serious it is." Hitler's next move was explosive. He dispatched one of his toughest generals, von Hanneken, to Denmark, with orders to initiate a reign of terror and install a puppet government headed by the leader of the Danish Nazi Party, Fritz Clausen. Dismayed, the government tried at once to mollify Hitler, offering to send Crown Prince Frederick to Berlin with an assurance of Denmark's "unchanged friendly feelings." Berlin preserved complete silence. The air was thick with rumors and everyone prepared for the worst; this war of nerves was intended to increase uneasiness.

On the morning of October 19, while taking his usual ride through the capital, the king was thrown from his horse and sustained serious injuries. According to one report, the horse was frightened by the noise of a train, but the king was

an experienced rider and trains did not pass at that hour.
Someone suggested that a German soldier deliberately frightened the horse. Whatever the cause, the king regained control
until, on reaching the Yacht Club, the horse broke into a wild
gallop. To avoid hurting anyone, the king pulled in the horse
with such force that it reared and he was thrown to the ground.
A nearby German SS guard hurried to his side. "Don't touch
me," shouted the monarch, "go away." A Danish waitress
rushed from a nearby restaurant, wiped the blood from his
face, and held his head in her lap until an ambulance arrived.
The king appeared to be recovering, but pneumonia soon set
in; by October 25 his condition had become critical and the
crown prince was named regent. Crowds collected in front of
the hospital every day to hear the news of his health. Slowly
the bulletins got more hopeful; by the end of the first week
in November, the king was pronounced out of danger.

Like the rest of the country, Monica and her family were
concerned about their king's health. "Today the weather is
dark and blowy in keeping with the sad news of King Christian's fall from his horse," Monica wrote in her monthly letter
to Brian Taylor. "The poor old gentleman is seventy and now
it appears that pneumonia has set in. Couldn't be more serious
at his age." She goes on to describe the improvements in her
newly rigged "temporary central-heating apparatus which
gives us a modicum of heat, providing all the double doors
in the enfilade of rooms are left open. It saves on wood, of
which luckily we have a certain amount, but who knows how
long this war is going to last?" Naturally Monica could not
mention her Resistance activities in her letters, but one senses
her good humor and new spirit. The bouts of domesticity came
as a relief from the tensions generated by her underground

work. "Do you remember our discussing *Out of Africa* and *Seven Gothic Tales?*" she asked in her letter to Taylor. "Well, when I was down in the author's neighborhood the other day, it was arranged by mutual friends that I should come in and pay her a visit later this year. I am very much looking forward to this. . . . I borrowed Erskine Caldwell's *Jackpot*—all his short stories in one volume. I dive into them at odd moments in between chores: they only take about ten minutes each to read! Now don't laugh: I am planning to read various books on socialism and instruct myself in this new 'creed,' which will be of great use to me one day. For I know that the world will be a changed place after the war, particularly here and in England. It will affect me personally very little, for I have lived the life of 'the man in the street' on and off for at least twenty years, but I wonder how our Barbara Huttons will take it. It will do them a world of good, says I."

In early December Monica was preoccupied with her older son Ivan's engagement to Hanne Basse, with whom he had been in love since the last winter. "Hanne is tall, with darkish auburn hair, a lovely figure, and the most beautiful dark blue eyes I have ever seen, with long dark lashes," Monica wrote Brian Taylor. "She is full of humor, sweet, kind, and generous, and we all adore her. She is about Varinka's age, a few months older. (Varinka will be twenty-one on February 9.) She helps my husband to garden when she is here, and generally slaves for him; she and Viggo are also very close. We are extremely lucky and it will be lovely to have Hanne in the family."

Christmas came with its traditional fir tree, roast goose with red cabbage and apples, ginger cakes, and rice pudding with cinnamon and one almond. The entire family gathered around the long dining-room table. Jorgen's mother, Bedste-moder, attended with her daughter Addi, Ivan brought Hanne, Inkie and Viggo returned from Copenhagen for the holidays. Afterward there was a party at Hardenberg, Heini's sumptuous home, where young and old enjoyed the last vestige of the good prewar life. As she lifted her champagne glass on New Year's Eve, Monica knew with instinctive certainty that the year about to begin would be crucial for her.

Seven

Life under the Nazis

WHILE MONICA was in Copenhagen discussing the problems
of safe houses on Lolland with Bobby Moltke, RAF Mosquito
bombers attacked the city's shipbuilding works, which produced engines for German U-boats. It was the first air raid
Copenhagen had experienced since the occupation. At five
o'clock in the afternoon, as the January night began to fall
over the city, the eight British planes, flying low to evade radar,
dropped their load of explosives and incendiary bombs on the
engine works at Christianshavn. From her hotel on Kleins-
gade, Monica could see the flames shooting up into the sky
and heard the violent detonations. The destruction, which was
nearly total, was made even more complete by the fact that
Danish explosives experts, who were ordered to defuse the
delayed-action bombs, cunningly omitted those which could
inflict damage on key workshops and drawing offices. The
German propaganda minister, Dr. Goebbels, "froze" the news
of the air raid for three days, then announced that a "terror
attack" had taken place and that British planes "had fired on
the Danish population." On seeing the markings of the air-

planes, many had excitedly waved greetings to the bombers, including Monica. She returned to Engestofte in a cheerful mood; things were really beginning to happen.

Rather recklessly, she carried a large suitcase full of copies of *Free Denmark* and *Information* to be distributed on Lolland by her network, knowing that possession of copies of the underground press was a punishable offense. German sentries, guarding the approach to the bridge between the islands of Zealand and Falster, stopped people at random to inspect the contents of their luggage, but Monica admitted she enjoyed this dangerous encounter. "I always manage to brazen it out," she said. "They stare at me, I look insolent and contemptuous, and they wave me on every time." Her tactics worked, but had she been caught it would have ended her Resistance work. Distributing underground papers was a small part of Monica's assignment. She was now the vital link between Hilmar Wulff and Erik Kiersgaard in their sabotage efforts. She also gave shelter to fugitives from the Danish and German police. Both actions were punishable by deportation to Germany. In March 1943 she was given important new responsibilities, coinciding with a new chapter in the history of occupied Denmark.

The defeat of the Germans at Stalingrad, their expulsion from North Africa after El Alamein, British and American air superiority with bombing raids deep inside Germany, the failure of the German submarine offensive in the North Atlantic, and the first Japanese reverses in the Pacific and the Far East led more and more Danes to reconsider the merits of neutrality. Wasn't the Allied cause the one to support now? The planners at SOE headquarters in London decided the time was ripe to build up the Resistance movement in Denmark. The January raid on Copenhagen's shipyards had been proposed by Ebbe Munck, the Danish newspaperman in Stockholm. Apart from its military value, its purpose was to show his compatriots that the price of appeasement was too high. SOE in London began to search for a leader who would volunteer to be parachuted into Denmark and take charge of this opposition. They found him in Flemming Muus, a thirty-six-year-old Dane of great courage. He had been working in Liberia when the war started and managed to reach London by ship from Monrovia, having paddled a dugout canoe along the West African coast for twelve days.

After extensive training in London, Muus was parachuted into Denmark on March 12, 1943. Equipped with false identity papers and authentic Danish clothing (including store labels), he landed in Jutland and the next morning proceeded by train to Copenhagen, where he met with his prearranged contact.

Muus recalled how he felt on the first morning in his native country and at his first sight of German soldiers: "From the eastern shore of Fyn one has to take a ferry to reach Zealand, on the far side of which stands Copenhagen. It was no joke getting on that ferry at Nyborg in Fyn. There were at least ten German sentries at the gangway, and they looked the passengers over very carefully, ready to arrest anyone who seemed the least bit suspicious. I went past them with my heart in my mouth. . . . And then we were away. At eight that night we arrived in Copenhagen. I felt I had come home at last, as I walked from the Central Station to the beer-and-sausage bar on the Town Hall Square." He had a clear-cut idea of his mission—to push Denmark fully into the Allied camp and erase the impression of a neutral nation. He longed for his country to be recognized as a full-fledged ally of the United States and Britain. In this respect his views were identical with Monica's. They were well aware that this meant undermining the legal government of the country, the Danish police, and some elements in the army and navy, all functioning under the protective cover of the Germans. Luckily the very clumsiness of the Germans was to resolve that problem.

Monica met Flemming Muus in late spring of 1943 through Bobby Moltke. Since his arrival, Muus had been concentrating on Jutland, the northernmost province of Denmark, which faced Norway, arranging for parachute drops of men and military supplies from England and their secret reception on the ground. "I had been so busy that I neglected the southern islands of Lolland and Falster," he recalls in his book, *The Spark and the Flame.* "However, we could not continue to neglect this important piece of Denmark. Lolland and Falster would become of vital importance on account of their geographical position in the event of a German retreat. It was time to begin. But I was not able to spare anyone for the job at the time: One day, as I talked to Bobby Moltke, he said that 'much would be gained' if he could put me in touch with Monica Wichfeld. He had known the family for years and Monica was in his confidence—one of the few people aware of his connection with the Resistance. . . . I at once agreed to a meeting."

Their first secret meeting took place at the Damehotellet in Copenhagen. "I was immediately aware that I was in the presence of a truly great personality. We discussed ways and means of founding groups and Mrs. Wichfeld without hesitation put the fields of Engestofte at our disposal for the reception of 'drops' from the air. With remarkable astuteness she suggested dropping containers into the Maribo Lake. They would have markers attached, so they could easily be found and retrieved when the time came. I was amazed, for I happened to know that something very similar was being planned in England at that very moment by some of our most brilliant RAF brains. This was one example of Mrs. Wichfeld's talent of instinctively putting her finger on a vital point. She was right, and in the course of the next eighteen months we received a large quantity of material in this way."

The result was that Monica Wichfeld was put in charge of building an organization on Lolland on the same lines as those in Jutland and Fyn. With the help of a well-trained paratrooper, whose alias was "Jacob," they would guide drops of containers, retrieve them, give shelter to the most wanted saboteurs, and hide them until they could be smuggled into Sweden. They would also receive and supervise transports of ammunition and high explosives, some of which would have to be concealed in the family house for weeks on end. Additional safe houses would be needed. Finally, one of the most wanted saboteurs, responsible for delaying an important transport of relief troops to Norway, who was being hunted by the German police, would be sent to Engestofte until his escape to Sweden could be arranged. "Mummy came back from Copenhagen beaming," recalled Inkie. "Bobby had introduced her to Mr. Miller (alias Flemming Muus), the CO parachutist in Denmark. He needed safe houses for wanted people and a lot of other things. Was she willing to be in charge? The answer I leave you to guess."

After the young saboteur whom Monica lodged in her best guest room, but whose name she was never told, had been spirited away to Sweden on a fishing boat via Bornholm, Muus sent her a message that one of his boys, Jacob Jensen (whose cover name was Jens Jacobsen), would shortly be on his way. He was to stay in the neighborhood and with Monica's help pinpoint likely places for the dropping of arms by parachute. He would also instruct local patriots in the use of firearms and the preparation of high explosives. Monica went to Copenhagen to meet a burly, thickset, fisherman-like type from Fyn. He had been on a Danish fishing trawler in the Persian Gulf when Denmark was first occupied, and made his way to England, where he had been trained in sabotage by the SOE. One look was enough to convince her she could not plausibly have him to stay at the house for a protracted period on such pretexts as friend, tutor, or even manservant. She asked Muus to defer his arrival for a day and went home to consult Hilmar Wulff. "I knew from experience," recalled Wulff, "that Mrs. Wichfeld was active in the underground movement, but I was not prepared for the huge strides she had made. After dinner we went for a walk in the park and Mrs. Wichfeld asked me straight out, 'Can you have a parachutist to stay?' Just recently word had come down to us from Communist HQ that we were to collaborate with everybody who was fighting the Germans and I did not hesitate to say, 'Yes, of course.' He was to be officially described as one of my wife's cousins."

Jacob came and was soon joined by Erik Kiersgaard, who arrived in a van from Copenhagen with cases full of arms and explosives. At a signal from Monica, who made sure they were not being observed, the cache was hauled through the park to the little private jetty on the lake and rowed across to Wulff's cottage, where the arms were buried in the woods.

Soon Monica was being approached by local young men from Maribo, who cautiously gave her to understand that they would like to offer their services to the cause. She had to find the right place for them to be trained; it did not take her long to decide that Pastor Marcussen was the ideal man to approach.

From the first days of her arrival at Engestofte, Monica had liked and admired Pastor Marcussen. He was an anachronism in a land where most people slavishly espoused progress. Denmark, though officially Lutheran, is not a religious country and Lolland was renowned for being heathen, in spite of its numerous early churches. The pastor was both mentally and physically a man outside his time—small, frail-looking, already touched by tuberculosis. His eyesight was poor, yet the first thing one noticed about him were his eyes—those of a fanatical believer, fervent and intense, Dürer eyes. On Sundays, standing in the richly carved pulpit of his church, dressed in a black cassock and Jacobean ruff, with his small pointed beard and piercing eyes, he exercised a powerful influence. His strong face and passionate commitment were apparent to his listeners. And he spoke in the most beautiful Danish, *Høj Dansk*, which, as Jorgen remarked, could be heard only at the Royal Theater or "in the highest society circles." Pastor Marcussen cared passionately about two things: his religion and freedom.

Monica and the pastor established a relationship of understanding and mutual trust. She was also deeply fond of Mrs. Marcussen, of Norwegian origin, who was quiet, modest, and reserved. This remarkable couple put the vast, secluded garden of the vicarage at Monica's disposal. No questions were asked; they were ready to help.

Another recruit to Monica's network was Gerner Nielsen, the director of the lunatic asylum at Sakskøbing, a small town a few miles beyond the vicarage. Gerner Nielsen was a tall, well-built man in his fifties, with a short gray crew cut and a commanding presence. Neither he nor his wife, a fair, blue-eyed Nordic woman, needed much persuasion to join the Resistance. The last recruit on Monica's team was young Hans Christian Hovmand, a popular veterinarian from Nykøbing on Falster. He was a friend of Erik Kiersgaard and with gasoline in short supply, his veterinary van was invaluable for transporting explosives and other forbidden cargo. The Nakskov shipyard, at the far end of the island of Lolland, had been targeted for sabotage, and high-explosive materials were being assembled at Engestofte. All this went on under the unsuspecting eyes of Jorgen de Wichfeld, who would have been horrified had he known what was being done under his roof.

"One day Erik turned up in a commercial van with the vet driving," recalled Inkie. "He asked whether he could leave a couple of suitcases with us. Jens was to fetch them later. Ivan, home for the weekend, and Viggo, down from his school, helped Erik carry the load to the attic. They complained we were all being treated like cloakroom attendants by Erik, 'a rude young man.' . . . Mummy and I, who of course had been expecting the consignment, laughed inwardly at their blindness and tried to humor them as well as we could. That night, after everyone had gone to bed, we crept out of the house, took the boat, and rowed across to Hilmar's house, where Jens was staying. They came back with us and fetched the suitcases, while we made sure there was nobody about watching us."

Most of that late spring and early summer Monica traveled regularly to Copenhagen under the pretext of visiting the dentist or seeing Viggo, but in reality to report to Flemming Muus, her controller-boss, at his secret command post. In early July last-minute complications prevented her from leaving Engestofte and keeping her appointment with Mr. Miller, as Muus was known. She decided to send Varinka instead. She wrote down her message to Muus, slipped it into the back of a compact, and asked Varinka to hand it to an elderly lady (code-named Daphne) at a certain hotel in Copenhagen. If Daphne was not available, Inkie was to contact Mr. Miller himself, but *only* as a last resort; Monica told her how to go about seeing him. Inkie, who was an enterprising, curious, and totally fearless girl, did not bother about Daphne but sought out the boss. They met and he was charmed. "The moment I saw her I decided that she was to be my wife," Flemming Muus recalled in *The Spark and the Flame*. It impressed Inkie to be in the presence of the man who could summon airplanes to come over with arms or arrange flights to Sweden at a moment's notice. She said he was between thirty-five and forty and a bit Chinese-looking (he had undergone a face-lift in England so as not to be recognized). "He wore large glasses and seemed to watch the world skeptically from behind them. Two scars descended from behind his ears to his jaw. He was dressed in a blue suit and to my utter amazement had a packet of Gold Flakes on the table. All Virginia cigarettes were worth their weight in gold in Denmark at the time and impossible to obtain." (Mr. Miller's may have come through the courtesy of the American Tobacco representatives in Copenhagen, who supplied them to the underground all through the war.)

Inkie was thrilled when Flemming Muus offered her the job of secretary to his assistant Professor Rantzau, head of the underground's propaganda department. Her job was to translate the leaflets received in the containers dropped from England. She did her job with great skill and two months later became Flemming Muus's secretary and assistant. She married him in June 1944. Resourceful and fearless, operating under the code name Kirsten, she made a contribution to the Resistance acknowledged in her country to this day. In late July, when Monica came up to Copenhagen, Inkie arranged for her to see *Desert Victory*, the film about Montgomery's victory at El Alamein, which had arrived from England by parachute. It was shown in a small projection room in the Palladium, Copenhagen's main cinema. The film was a marvelous boost to all their spirits.

Denmark was not yet "the fuel that would spontaneously burst into flame" that Churchill hoped for, but sabotage and underground activities increased. "Our task is made immeasurably easier every time an Allied victory is announced," reported Ronald Turnbull, the SOE intelligence man in one of his dispatches to London. During the summer of 1943, as arms and explosives poured into the country, between fifty and eighty acts of sabotage were carried out each night. Newly arrived paratroopers taught young recruits, who in turn started blowing up vital targets like railway bridges. This prevented German troops from being moved. Factories making parts for German U-boats were also prime targets. In Jutland, where the railway was vital for the German army traveling between Norway and the fatherland, vital sections of the track were destroyed nightly.

Every evening at the shipyards of Odense there were clashes between German soldiers and the local people, whom the Germans now complained of as "unfriendly." Into this explosive situation came one of the SOE instructors, Jens Carlsen ("Lard"). The German minesweeper *Linz*, commissioned two and a half years earlier, had been delayed by workers' slowdowns. Now it was ready. The shipyard workers, lined up on the dock for a photograph, had in their midst a saboteur with an SOE-supplied limpet mine in his lunch box. With the Wehrmacht brass due to arrive for the launching ceremony, the *Linz* was blown up. When General von Hanneken, the commander in chief in Denmark, sent in armed troops, the people of Odense went on strike. This pattern was now being repeated all over the country—sabotage, German reaction, general strike. This of course put the Danish police, who had to arrest the saboteurs and deliver them into German hands, in a very difficult situation. It also pushed the government itself to the wall. The situation was becoming explosive and things were working up to a climax.

This was exactly what Flemming Muus had intended. Since his arrival he had managed to get many different elements—ordinary citizens, army and navy people, farmers, workers, Communists, clergy—working together smoothly throughout the country. The paratroopers under his command were a compact and orderly team, very well disciplined. Arms and supplies were dropped regularly and successfully retrieved. The favored reception points were well-defined open spaces and manor-house fields, like Engestofte's, easily identifiable from the air. Parachutes and other "dangerous litter" were rapidly disposed of on the ground: a parachute retrieved from Maribo Lake ended up as a christening robe for one of the Engestofte farmers' children, the fine quality of its silk much appreciated in wartime.

Monica was in full control of her operation, thankful that neither Jorgen nor her two boys had the slightest inkling of what was going on. She had taken a room over the servants' quarters and turned it into her sitting room, where she spent several hours each day. She gave a plausible reason for her move, explaining to her husband that it was difficult for her to write letters, sew, and work on accounts in the main part of the house, where she was being constantly interrupted. She needed a study. This room had direct access to an outside staircase. The setup enabled her to see her Resistance colleagues in privacy. Her family left her alone, and deliberately avoided that part of the house. Engestofte, a large, sprawling house with a number of outside staircases, was ideal for quick escapes. Above Monica's bedroom were two floors of attics, to which she kept a key in a large painted wooden box on her desk. Thus several people could be hidden in the attic bedrooms for days without anyone being aware of them. "How she managed to feed them without the servants being alerted, I do not know," one of her sons stated.

The handling and distribution of weapons and explosives also presented difficulties. They had to be rowed across the lake, two miles wide, to the hideaway cottage, where Hilmar Wulff and other members of her group were living. Jacob, Erik Kiersgaard, and Hans Hovmand, the vet, assisted by an ever-increasing number of volunteers, were entrusted with the distribution. But emergencies kept occurring. Many nights, long after the family had gone to bed, Monica would slip out of the house carrying a large bag of explosives. A lonely figure silhouetted against the shoreline, she walked carefully down the terrace steps to the little pier from which she rowed her dangerous cargo across the lake. Her muffled oars and greased ruddocks made little noise. She moved silently on the water, like a ghost. Some nights were blowy and rainy, but on others, when the moon shone and the waters were still, the beauty of the lake overwhelmed her. It was her old "pathway to the moon" from the days of her childhood in Ireland with Jack. "On such nights I could have gone on rowing forever," she said. The wooden boat was heavy and awkward to maneuver alone and she often missed the help of Varinka, who was making her own contribution to the cause. "Why do you have such calluses on your hands?" her husband asked her one day as she was pouring tea in the red sitting room. She blamed them on the lack of good soap and the wartime shortage of hand creams; Jorgen accepted her explanation.

Monica's older son, Ivan, was getting married in Copenhagen in August and the bride's parents wanted it to be the social event of the season. "Ivan comes home tomorrow for a week to pack up all his belongings and get his clothes in order for his final departure from the nest," Monica wrote Brian Taylor. "I have always imagined that his marriage would be the end of my responsibilities as a mother, but I have just been informed that his future wife has no idea about practical things, like cooking, sewing, or mending, so he intends to continue sending home his shirts and clothes to be mended, washed, and looked after. . . . It is going to be a great occasion; about eighty people in church in full evening dress, tails, and gala uniforms at 5:30 in the afternoon—Danish custom! Then dinner at the leading hotel at 6:30 and about a hundred of the bridal couple's young friends to dance after dinner." A week later she added: "P.S. The wedding went off splendidly; it was attended by various members of the royal family and a glittering assembly of Copenhagen's *beau monde*, who in the midst of wartime gloom all relished the occasion to dress up and get their jewels out of the bank's safes. I sat between Prince Axel of Denmark and my mother-in-law in the first row and had a good view of my dear son, who looked exceedingly handsome. His bride is a beauty, one of the prettiest girls I've ever seen. . . . It was of course a Lutheran ceremony, strictly following the old-established Danish ritual. I missed the lovely hymns I have been used to since childhood, particularly 'Lead Kindly Light' and all the other music and the singing I associate with our English weddings. I also found it quite strange to have to appear in evening clothes and full makeup at 4:30 p.m. while brilliant summer light poured through the stained-glass windows; I would have much preferred candlelight." Pretty, twenty-one-year-old Varinka, by then deep in her dangerous work, recalled the ball following her brother's wedding. "Little did I know that it would be the last time I was to see Mummy at her loveliest in a beautiful evening dress, long diamond earrings, eyes shining, dancing her incomparable Viennese waltz with Daddy."

The wedding over, Monica returned to the underground activities on Lolland and Falster. She was much needed, for in the week after her return the strongest wave of sabotage began in Denmark. Muus's telegram to London warning that "if the present pace of resistance continued, the Huns would have to take drastic steps" was answered with a clear: "Go right ahead." There were renewed strikes and disturbances at Odense, Ålborg, Århus, and in practically all the towns in Jutland and Fyn. The railway system in Jutland was disrupted in 189 places and the shipyard at Nakskov was put out of commission by Erik Kiersgaard and his group. At Odense the directors of the Danish Foreign Office and of the Ministry of Justice, the Minister of Labor, the Borgmester of the town, even the union leaders pleaded with the workers to go back to their jobs, but their pleas were in vain. Anti-Nazi demonstrations were getting out of control. Streets in most Danish towns were now dominated by hardened frontline SS troops, putting down scuffles and firing guns. On the morning of August 24, 1943, a team of five men, trained by Flemming Muus, were ordered to blow up the Forum, Copenhagen's largest public hall. They did it that very afternoon, in broad daylight. For Hitler it was the last straw. Four days later the Danish government faced a German ultimatum.

The Germans asked that a state of emergency be declared, that all demonstrations be banned, as well as all gatherings of more than five people, that strict censorship be imposed, military courts sentencing people to death for sabotage and for sheltering saboteurs. The prime minister knew the only thing they could do was to reject the ultimatum. The Danish government had been humiliated long enough; the next step was mass resignation. There would now be no government. Hitler had taken charge; *they* were the enemy. This cleared the air, and it was exactly what the Resistance had hoped for.

The Germans struck in the night, after General von Hanneken had made thorough preparations. At four o'clock in the morning of August 29 he gave the signal for Operation Blitz. In pouring rain and darkness, attacks were carried out against Danish military establishments throughout the country. Everywhere officers and men were interned and military material confiscated. The Danish navy, however, reacted swiftly and began to scuttle its ships. Within hours twenty-nine vessels lay at the bottom of the harbor; all other ships were ordered to make for Sweden. Denmark was now a subjugated nation under German dictatorship. The king's palace was placed under surveillance and the sovereign and his family were told that their movements were restricted. The king remained under virtual house arrest until the end of the war.

Flemming Muus had gone into hiding a few days before the fatal day. "To avoid a probable German sweep, I checked into a private clinic (a home for expectant mothers) and got

a room facing the intersection of Gothersgade and Kronprin-
sensgade," he recalls in *The Spark and the Flame*. "Early in
the morning I was awakened by crashes from the Holmens
Canal area. I did not know at that moment that it was Admiral
Vedel keeping his promise that he never again would let a
ship of our fleet fall into German hands without resistance. I
heard shots and could see flashes in Kongens Have. Fighting
was going on. The Wehrmacht had struck, but this time there
was no surrender; vessels of our Navy which could not get
away and shape a route for Sweden were all scuttled. . . .
There was no doubt about it: the spirit of 1864, when the
Danes had fought a ferocious battle against the Germans in
Southern Jutland, was reborn that night."

In September, much to Monica's regret, Hilmar Wulff
had to move to Copenhagen. On a gray, blowy morning,
shortly after his departure, Monica, looking out the window
of her room, saw the sturdy figure of Mrs. Kann, the wife of
the real-estate agent, hurriedly making her way up the drive,
agitated and nervous. It turned out that friends of the Kanns,
a Jewish family from Copenhagen, a mother and three teenage children, were in need of a hiding place in the country.
The roundup of Danish Jews had begun. The Gerner Nielsens
at the asylum offered to take two of the children, but Mrs.
Kauffman and her daughter Hanne were desperate. Mrs.
Kann, who was sheltering other Jewish refugees, hoped that
they could all be dispatched to Sweden as soon as possible.
Monica was aware that the Resistance movement forbade
her to involve herself in the concealment and escape of Danish
Jews, for fear of jeopardizing the existing network. It was
thought that there were enough humane Danish people who
would help without running the same risks. So her first re-

action was negative. But a few hours later Mrs. Kann returned to plead again—they *really* had nowhere to go. Monica agreed to hide them, but they would have to live in the servants' wing, pass themselves off as staff, wear blue maids' uniforms in the event of a German inspection of the house, and above all promise not to communicate with the outside world by letter or telephone. Mrs. Kauffman and Hanne gratefully accepted the invitation.

For years Jews in German-occupied territories had been persecuted and subjected to mass extermination as the Final Solution, but in Denmark they had been unharmed. Hitler needed the cooperation of the Danish government for economic and strategic reasons. Anti-Semitism had been unacceptable in Denmark since the seventeenth century, when Christian V refused permission for a Jewish ghetto to be established in the capital. During the early occupation, whenever a German official brought up "the Jewish question" with the king, he coldly answered: "We have no Jewish question in this country. There are only my people." On another occasion he was reported to have stated to the German ambassador: "Since we Danes do not consider ourselves inferior to the Jews, we have no Jewish problem." But on August 29, 1943, Denmark became another Hitler fief and the Führer, enraged by the rejection of his ultimatum, called for the immediate arrest of the country's seven thousand Jews. The *Warthegau*, a merchant ship, was sent from Hamburg and lay at anchor in the Copenhagen harbor, ready to transport them to concentration camps.

There followed a unique chapter in the history of occupied Europe: another Dunkirk was enacted, as an entire nation rallied to the assistance of its persecuted minority and saved it. Of the nearly seven thousand Jews more than sixty-five hundred were rescued and transported to Sweden, where they were given asylum. The unfortunate few who were too ill or too old to be moved were rounded up and deported to Theresienstadt, a concentration camp on the border of Germany and Czechoslovakia, where most of them survived the war.

Hitler's order for the deportation of the Jews reached Denmark on September 18 and was received with dismay by the Reich's plenipotentiary, Dr. Werner Best, who argued that it would dramatically increase the existing tension in the country. One of his assistants, G. F. Duckwitz, a pronounced anti-Nazi, was appalled by this development and, with Governor Best's knowledge, went to Stockholm to warn the Swedish government of the impending tragedy. On his return he leaked the news of the roundup, which was fixed for October 2, Rosh Hashanah, the Jewish New Year. The head of the Jewish community, the High Court Advocate C. B. Henriques, was able to warn his people in time. Overnight thousands of Jewish families vanished, hidden away in warehouses, asylums, and hospitals all over Denmark. When the first raids began to take place, the Gestapo found few Jews in their homes; some of them had not left because they "simply could not believe that harm could come to them in Denmark."

Overnight a gigantic rescue operation was mounted. The combined forces of the underground, Baltic fishermen, and hundreds of average Danish families succeeded in housing, hiding, and transporting fugitives. Fishing boats, coasters, and even rowboats were used to smuggle them across the Kattegat. The Swedes stood ready on the other side to grant them temporary asylum. Some refugees were transshipped in midstream to Swedish trawlers. In one village nearly a thousand

Jewish people were spirited away from its little harbor secluded among the dunes, with the fishermen's church converted into a waiting room. At one moment, fearing that the
Gestapo were approaching, refugees hid under the rafters.
"We were huddled in the roof, waiting for darkness and a
boat to Sweden," one refugee recalled. "As the hours passed,
temperatures dropped to near-freezing; there was no heat or
light; no one dared speak. Through a window we could actually see the coast of Sweden; earlier that day fifty of us had
passed safely across to freedom." Their turn eventually came
and they were rescued.

The Kauffman family, hiding at Engestofte and the Gerner Nielsen asylum, were among those successfully shipped
to Sweden. Monica had had some difficulty with Mrs. Kauffman, who, in danger of her life, was incongruously worried
about some clothes she had left in Copenhagen and tried,
despite her promise, to mail letters to her maid in town. Luckily they were intercepted and the danger of discovery averted.
The four wanted to travel together as a family, presenting an
additional complication, but Monica was able to arrange
transport. This is how Hanne Kauffman described her last
day on Lolland: "October 8. In the middle of the afternoon
a car drove up and came to a halt outside. We peeped anxiously from behind the curtains. . . . I felt as giddy as I had
on the day, more than a week ago, when I walked home from
school and heard the news of the impending pogrom. . . . My
brother and my sister were pale but composed, but my mother
seemed to have shrunk during that last week. Her gray eyes
were sunken, she had aged. . . . We didn't talk much during
the ride across Lolland. We looked out the windows at the
beautiful autumn colors, like a painted landscape. . . . We
proceeded in a convoy of cars to the tiny little harbor at Hest-

naes on the Baltic and on to Sweden." By the end of October
95 percent of the Jewish population had reached Sweden. Dr.
Werner Best, tongue-in-cheek, for he hated Himmler and his
gang, reported to Berlin: "Anti-Jewish action in Denmark
carried out without incident. As of today, Denmark can be
regarded as free of Jews." This did not endear him to Hitler
or to Adolf Eichmann, the notorious hunter of the Jews, but
other urgent matters were pressing on the Führer.

"You've never in your life seen such an October as we
have had here," Monica wrote to Brian Taylor in her regular
letter to his POW camp. "Denmark is acting like my beloved
Italy, trying to persuade me to stay here forever. . . . We lunch
out on the terrace overlooking the lake every day, the lawn is
a yellow carpet of fallen linden leaves, the flaming woods are
reflected in the lake, and there is a stillness unheard of in this
country, as if nature were holding its breath listening to the
sounds of guns over the water." For people who live in southern climes, it is hard to imagine the effect a spell of unbroken
fine weather, lasting week after week, has on inhabitants of
a northern region, used to intermittent cold and rain. It creates
an illusion of unreality, a dreamlike feeling of being sus-
pended in time. Monica, ever alert to the demands of her
work and with her mind concentrated on signals from the
BBC, found it hard to relate this arcadian weather to the
violence and bloodshed all around her. Under the eternal blue
sky the sun shone on the terrace, where lunch and tea were
being served every day, facing the lake, where the last wisteria
flowers were blooming. As the days became shorter and the
evenings cooler, they began to hear the distant thud of bombs
and the Allied bombers overhead. "Turning out the lights and
opening the curtains, we could see the fiery red glow to the

southeast, as Hamburg burned," recalled Viggo. "In the morning the sunlit lawns were littered with strips of silver, backed with black. We had no idea of their purpose and supposed they were cast by bombers to confuse the German searchlights. We had not yet heard about radar."

Jorgen was often away visiting various friends, and Monica spent many evenings talking to Viggo, who was home preparing for his architectural exams. "Looking back with hindsight," he recalls, "it is obvious that she must have expected something to happen. She went to Copenhagen and made her will, sorted personal papers, and, meticulously tidy as always, brought all her accounts up to date. During our long evenings by the fire, I found her anxious to communicate her thoughts, her experiences, and some of her frustrated ambitions to someone who she knew cared for her. . . . For the first time I found her willing to talk about her brother Jack, killed in the First World War. I have always known that her deep-seated hatred of German military aggression was closely bound with his death on the Somme. In the past, whenever Jack's name came up in the conversation, my mother would leave the room, unable to hear his name mentioned. That particular evening, however, when I inadvertently asked her, she got up and climbed the little staircase which connected the library to her bedroom. She came down with some letters in her hand and began to read them to me; they were charming, young, lighthearted letters, and Jack's obvious adoration of his sister shone through them. At the bottom of the pile were three unopened envelopes, which she slit with her sewing scissors and read to me in her distinctive contralto voice. 'They arrived after his death,' she explained. 'It is only now, when you and Ivan have reached his age, that I can for the first time utter his name without crying.' "

*   *   *

Pastor Marcussen, Hans Hovmand, Gerner Nielsen, and the others all had their allocated tasks. The burly Jacob came and went. When the master of the house encountered him he shrugged his shoulders. Jorgen described him as one of "our tenant's [Wulff's] queer, artistic friends." It never crossed his mind to inquire about Jacob's identity. Jacob was good at teaching the ever-increasing number of new recruits how to wait at night on the lonely heaths, to signal the low-flying RAF aircraft with electric torches, to gather the tons of materials that came cascading down in parachutes, and to spirit their cargo away before they were spotted. Jacob traveled around the islands distributing explosives and training recruits in sabotage. Following Flemming Muus's instructions, he kept in touch with Monica, his controller, and through her with Pastor Marcussen, Gerner Nielsen, Hans Hovmand, and their latest adherent, Wilhelm Grandt, editor of the Maribo paper.

Jacob was meticulous in carrying out orders, his work was good, and Monica had no specific reason to reproach him. And yet of all her collaborators he was the only one who made her feel occasionally doubtful. Working in the underground calls for absolute and mutual trust. It is a game played for high stakes, for the lives of all the participants are involved. She would have found it hard to explain why she had reservations about Jacob. Was it because he had roamed the world as an adventurer, a person for whom excitement appeared to be an end in itself? She thought that his moral standards were elastic, and he did not strike her as particularly patriotic or idealistic. She noticed how keen he was to receive the money she disbursed from the funds Muus provided. Jacob was tough, incontestably brave, well trained, and had passed SOE's scrutiny in London. Yet there was something about him that worried her. Bravery, she knew, does not always mean probity or strength of character. "How would Jacob stand up under Gestapo questioning, perhaps torture?" she asked Muus during one of their talks in Copenhagen. Flemming had no ready answer, but he hoped that in such an event Jacob would follow the manual of instructions, swallow the cyanide pill all agents carried, and foil his captors.

Not all agents were invariably heroic. Some had taken the job because it carried an officer's commission and the pay of a British army officer. Others were opportunists who squandered the large sums of money they were entrusted with. One agent went on a drinking spree in Copenhagen and boasted to chance acquaintances about his "secret work." He disobeyed an SOE order to return to Sweden and had to be liquidated by the underground. In December 1943, Flemming Muus decided to send Jacob to Jutland for a fortnight to help Ole Geisler, the brilliant Resistance leader in that part of the country. Jacob, a radio operator named Kai Lund, and Henrik Ibsen, a Norwegian parachutist who had recently arrived, were together in a safe house at Århus. Whether they had been drinking is not clear, but Jacob, in defiance of all security precautions, made several long-distance express calls to Randers. These calls were invariably tapped by the Germans, and it did not take the Gestapo much time to track down the three parachutists. The Nazis arrived at the Århus flat ten strong and arrested them. In spite of being well armed, Jacob and his companions surrendered without a fight.

Ibsen, having just arrived, was worthless to them and got off lightly. But Kai Lund, as a radio operator, was valuable prey and the Gestapo got much information out of him, including codes. He and Jacob were singled out for harsh treatment and were undoubtedly threatened with torture. The result for the Resistance was catastrophic. In the course of the next few weeks the names of forty-four people, all prominent in the underground movement, were revealed. Among them of course were Monica and her group. As Svend Truelsen put it, "Willpower and strength of character cannot be learned at any training school. It was tragic that it should have been the highly trained parachutists who gave away to the Germans more than any ordinary citizen unwittingly might have done."

Flemming Muus was in London at the time, but news of Jacob's arrest reached Monica through channels. No one knew how much the Germans had learned, but Monica, doubting the man as she did, had a sense of foreboding. She knew Jacob was not a Pastor Marcussen or an Eric Kiersgaard. "I have been so very happy lately," she told Viggo in October. "Something is bound to happen, I feel." Now she expected to be arrested at any moment, yet refused to take steps to avoid it. She could have been smuggled to Sweden through one of their well-established escape routes, but she rejected the idea as inconceivable. How could she leave her husband, Engestofte, and her children to the inevitable German reprisals that would follow? And there was perhaps something more: this most independent of women had always had a horror of old age and a fear of becoming a burden on others. Jorgen called it "Monica's obsession." "I am not a religious person," she once confided to a friend, "but having lived my life 'at a gallop' I ask God to let me finish it on a high note."

Being Irish, Monica was also a fatalist and superstitious. This had its source in her childhood on Lough Erne. Years earlier, in the heady twenties, Monica had visited a fortune-teller in Lausanne, at the height of her love affair with Reventlow. Madame Rédard had impressed her by describing the previous years of her life in accurate detail. She told Monica she would die "just before you reach fifty." Somewhat improbably, for she was a woman of intelligence, Monica believed her.

After the capture of the three parachutists at Århus, Ole Geisler had to leave Jutland to escape being caught. The heroic Hvidsten group, led by Marius Fiil and his family, who had been receiving men and supplies from Britain for over a year, stuck to their posts and continued to operate until they were captured in March 1944. Flemming Muus, having flown to London in December for discussions with the SOE, narrowly escaped death on his return, when his aircraft was spotted and shot down by a German night fighter. He landed safely by parachute and made his way back to Copenhagen, much to Varinka's joy. Monica's Resistance work stopped temporarily. She was living in an unreal limbo, not knowing exactly what the Gestapo knew.

The house was full. Ivan and Hanne arrived for their first Christmas at Engestofte, Viggo had a long holiday from his studies, Inkie arrived from Copenhagen "bursting with things to tell Mummy in private." She was being wooed ardently by Flemming Muus and was about to give in and accept his proposal.

On January 4, 1944, Kai Munk, the famous Danish playwright and clergyman, was abducted by the Nazis from his vicarage amid the dunes of West Jutland and found dead in a roadside ditch. He had preached a New Year's sermon condemning the occupation and urging his compatriots to commit sabotage. Munk was the victim of the new reign of terror ordered by the Führer. From now on until the liberation, murders and reprisals for sabotage would follow Resistance operations in quick succession.

On the day of Kai Munk's murder, Pastor Marcussen called at Engestofte. He asked to see Monica alone. Jorgen was away shooting, and they had tea in the peaceful green drawing room overlooking the lake. Monica waited for the pastor to speak and Marcussen later recorded what he said: "I told her that the parachutist she had harbored and who had recently been arrested had told the Gestapo *everything*. She remained absolutely calm. She smothered the flame underneath the teapot with a long silver snuffer and then fixed me with those tranquil, gray-green eyes of hers. I made an urgent, impassioned plea for her to escape, while there was still time. '*You* go,' she replied. I told her that was not the point; it was *she* who was in mortal danger. Sooner or later the Gestapo would surround the house and arrest her. 'I'm staying,' she replied. I asked her why. 'There are many reasons, of course, but let me say that, as I have joined the struggle for Denmark, I am willing to pay the price.' There was nothing more I could say and I went home with a heavy heart. It was the last time I saw her."

Eight

Arrest and Trial

ON JANUARY 13, 1944, snow lay thick on the ground and the temperature was well below freezing. Monica was in a deep sleep when, at five o'clock in the morning, the Gestapo abruptly burst into her bedroom, brandishing revolvers. They had forced the front door and ordered the terrified old cook to lead them upstairs. Monica awoke to find them standing by her four-poster bed, two heavily armed men in mackintoshes, with fedora hats pulled down over their eyes—"a cross between a nightmare and a gangster movie," as she told a fellow prisoner. They ordered her to get up instantly and to put on warm clothes, as she would be going on a long trip, and stood guard by her door while she dressed. Pulling the curtains aside on the wintry dawn, she could see the outlines of the great bare lime trees in the park silhouetted against the snow-covered lawns. Behind each tree stood a helmeted German soldier, machine gun at the ready, pointed toward the house. It was obvious that all escape routes were cut off. Monica dressed very slowly, with deliberate care, then went down to her small red sitting room, connected to her bedroom by a spiral staircase. She ordered the cook to light a fire and prepare breakfast. Her son Viggo appeared; he had been roughly pulled out of bed, made to dress under supervision, and marched down, hands over his head. "The house was freezing," he recalls, "as none of the large china stoves on the ground floor had yet been lit; everywhere there were men opening chests of drawers, writing tables, antique cupboards, and dumping the contents on the floor. I was led to my mother's sitting room. She was already there, fully dressed, immaculately turned out in a brown tweed shooting suit, cashmere sweater, woollen stockings, and highly polished brown brogues. She was calm, totally self-possessed, as if nothing unusual were happening. In the manner of a perfect hostess she turned to the various Gestapo who were now crowding the room and asked what they fancied for breakfast—tea, or perhaps ersatz coffee? Aware of the irony, they declined. One of them, who had been ferreting around, found a pile of maps under a marble console; each city captured by the Allies was ringed in red. "You are obviously pro-Allies?" he asked in a menacing tone. Looking him straight in the eye, through a wisp of cigarette smoke, Monica replied calmly: "Two of my brothers are fighting in the British army, a third was killed on the Somme in the First World War. What do you expect me to be, pro-German?" and she laughed.

At this point Jorgen Wichfeld was led in—in country tweeds, a monocle, an indignant expression on his face. He too had been abruptly awakened, pulled out of bed, and made to stand with hands up over his head. He turned to the assembled Gestapo: What on earth did they think they were doing in his house at such an hour? His controlled anger and outrage were so obviously genuine that the Germans were caught by surprise and some words of apology were mumbled.

Breakfast arrived; Monica took her place presiding over the silver tea tray, while the fire was lit in the large porcelain stove. But the Gestapo men announced that it was time to go. Going upstairs to wash her hands, followed by the ever-present Gestapo, Monica saw one of the agents in her bedroom opening the miniature leather suitcase where she kept her jewelry. With a lightning movement, so very characteristic of her, she slammed the lid shut, giving the man's fingers a nasty pinch, picked it up, and twirled the combination lock, so it could not be opened unless forced.

They were loaded into one of the two black tarpaulin-covered trucks waiting outside, three members of the family and two servants, surrounded by soldiers front and back, all guns pointing at them. One of the guns loomed uncomfortably close to Monica's face; without hesitation she seized the barrel and turned it downward. "Young man," she said in her fluent German, "you are a soldier, but you obviously have never been taught how to handle a gun. You should never point it at people; it might go off." There was a silence, then, as if by order, all the guns were lowered. She turned to one of the officers in charge and asked in a light, conversational tone, "I assume you are proposing to take us to some isolated spot to put a bullet in the back of our necks and dump our bodies in the nearest ditch, as your colleagues have just done with Pastor Kai Munk?" The officer, a Wehrmacht type, different from the Nazi inquisitors, appeared almost hurt by her words and protested, assuring her that German soldiers never committed such atrocities. "I am glad to hear it," she retorted. "It's a pity that everybody in Denmark believes that this was your doing."

As the sinister black truck with its prisoners, followed by a Gestapo staff car, drove down the long elm avenue to the main road, Monica turned to look back at the neo-classical façade of Engestofte, framed by the giant old trees, under a clear, aquamarine Nordic sky. It was to be her last view of the house that she had loved and had fought so hard to preserve for her sons.

Crossing the main Maribo road, the cars now proceeded north toward the candy-pink church at Vaabensted and drove into the courtyard of the rectory. Monica's heart gave a jolt; if only she could have warned her friend of what was coming. Three armed men went into the house, but after a very long time they came out without Pastor Marcussen. Having heard of the dawn raid on Engestofte through one of his parishioners, he was prepared. Before the Gestapo arrived he escaped through the back door across the frozen fields of sugar beet, while his wife calmly played Schubert on the piano in the drawing room, denying all knowledge of his whereabouts. She saved his life.

The next stop was the lunatic asylum at Sakskøbing; the Gestapo had been there already for some time. This is how Gerner Nielsen describes his arrest: "While my house was being thoroughly searched, the Germans had given orders that things should carry on normally at the asylum, and that all telephone calls were to be answered by them. But when the phone rang I quickly picked up the receiver. It was Pastor Marcussen before the Gestapo came to his house." (He wanted to tell Nielsen that a raid was in progress on Engestofte.) "I abruptly broke off the conversation, so as to make him realize that there was also something wrong at my end and to warn him. 'I'm being interviewed, I can't talk to you.' I slammed the receiver down before a furious agent grabbed it."

Nielsen joined the prisoners in the truck. "Conversation

is forbidden," soldiers shouted. "Anyone attempting to escape will be shot." Several more men were brought in, including Wilhelm Grandt of the Maribo paper.

Monica was lost in thought; she was trying to figure out a way of communicating with her husband, who sat opposite, and prepare him for what might happen to her. She had not yet been formally interrogated, but from what the Gestapo officer had said, she realized that they were extremely well-informed and that it would be impossible to shake off their accusations. It was obvious that Jacob had not spared any details. As they passed through Maribo, their local town, Jorgen de Wichfeld, noticing that the staff car carrying the Gestapo officers was well behind them, asked the soldiers to stop the convoy in the square for a moment so he could buy cigarettes for his wife. Monica was a heavy smoker and the strain of the day made her craving even more intense. The manager of the grocery store, Qvade's, rushed out of his shop with two cartons from his precious reserves; Monica looked at him and at her husband with gratitude.

The convoy then moved on toward Nakskov, the westernmost point of the island of Lolland. As they passed by the estate of their friends the Frijses, with its tidy, immaculate cottages and large Victorian Gothic-style house set close to the main road, Monica whispered to Viggo, "If Irene Frijs were to look out of her bedroom window at this moment, she would get the shock of her life," and they both smiled.

At the barracks, down by the harbor of Nakskov near the docks (only recently heavily damaged by explosives placed by Monica's team), Monica was interrogated twice by two different sets of agents. "When my mother came back into the room after the second interrogation, I sensed that the situation

was grave," recalls Viggo. "But outwardly she remained unperturbed."

Gerner Nielsen recalled how he was cross-examined: they
asked what he knew of Mrs. Wichfeld. "Everyone knows her
on Lolland," he replied. "She is also on the board of the
asylum." "Have you ever been to Engestofte?" "Yes, my wife
and I have been there several times for dinner or for tea. Mrs.
Wichfeld also came to the asylum for the board meetings."
"But have you ever discussed war or sabotage with her?" "Of
course we have. None of us discusses anything else since you
occupied our country some years ago." "How long have you
known Pastor Marcussen?" "About eight years." "What is his
attitude?" "I don't think there is any doubt that he is anti-
German, and quite frankly so am I." They then went on to
ask him about the Jews. *"Sie haben zwei Juden versteckt."*
("You've hidden two Jews.") "No, I didn't hide them; they
lived quite openly in my house for all to see." "But if the
Gestapo had come, would you have hidden them?" "Of
course I would have." "What did you do with them?" "Oh,
they have gone on to Sweden." "How?" "I don't know who
organized the escape, but I expect they got there like the
others. . . . It is all well behind us now." Nielsen was pleased
when his gardener, Carl Johanssen, who was the next to be
cross-examined, was only severely admonished and then released. "I wondered whether Mrs. Wichfeld had found some
way to warn her husband of what might be happening to her,"
he recalled. "Later, as it was icy-cold, Mrs. Wichfeld lent me
her beautiful cashmere rug, which several of us were grateful
for, as we shared it during the drive to Copenhagen in the
truck."

As the interminable day drew to a close, Jorgen, Viggo,

and the two servants were told that they were free to return home, but that they would be keeping "the Lady"; she was to be taken to Copenhagen that evening. Jorgen went up to the Wehrmacht officer and extracted a promise that his wife would be driven to the city in a staff car and not in a truck. Jorgen and Viggo said their goodbyes and left her, desperate in their own helplessness. Jorgen's mind was of course swirling with hundreds of questions, to which Monica had had no time to provide answers.

It was dark when the convoy pulled up in front of Vestre Faengsel, the West Prison, a gloomy Victorian building which loomed like a forbidding presence in the center of Copenhagen. They were told to line up, faces to the wall, and after an hour's wait were led to their individual confinement places. Monica's new home was a 10 × 6-foot damp, dark cell with a tiny barred window up near the ceiling and a bunk covered with a thin, well-worn mattress; there was a chamber pot underneath. The next day she was interrogated for eight hours, but divulged nothing.

While his wife was being taken to prison in Copenhagen, Jorgen, with Viggo and the two servants, walked to the local station in the snow and after a long wait managed to get a train to Maribo. Viggo, with great presence of mind, telephoned the family lawyer from a public booth and in careful telephone-speak asked him to tell Inkie what had happened; she ought to take instant cover. "It was late evening by the time we got home," recalled Viggo. "After being fetched from the Maribo station, we stopped in the red brick quadrangle on the farm, where Mrs. Knudsen, our tenant's wife, received us in her warm, comfortable house and produced a welcome hot meal. It was agreed that my father would spend the night there in case the Gestapo returned—also because our house had remained unheated all day. In his complete innocence my father couldn't understand what had happened and was in a state of shock. Several times during dinner he assured us that it was nothing and 'Monica will surely be back tomorrow.' Just as well that he did not know the real truth, for it would have completely shattered him. He went on living in a state of illusion; I did not have the heart to disabuse him."

Having made arrangements for his father, Viggo walked alone to the empty house. It was in darkness and of course very cold, the rooms still littered with the contents of the emptied drawers. "My first priority," he recalls, "was to go up to the attic and fetch a revolver, which my mother had managed to tell me she had hidden among the chaff which was used to insulate the pipes on the very top attic floor. I found it and put it in a basket full of grain, which my father always kept in the front hall to feed the pheasants in the park during the winter. I let myself out of the house and walked carefully through the snow to the little dock by the lakeshore, broke the ice with an ax, and threw the gun into the lake. I went back, locked the massive front door, and went up to my mother's room to pack some things I thought she would need in prison. I desperately wanted to be useful and to find an occupation to distract my mind from the disaster which had overtaken the person I cared for most in the world. I was also concerned about my sister's safety and wondered whether our lawyer understood the urgency of my telephone message."

Monica's large corner bedroom was in total confusion. Where order had always reigned, piles of embroidered underclothes and nightdresses, sweaters, handkerchiefs, bags, shoes, and assorted papers lay in heaps on the floor. Every drawer, it seemed, had been opened. Viggo slowly began to collect warm clothing, medicine, toilet articles, anything he thought might be of use or comfort to her in the prison, and packed them in a suitcase. He then found her jewelry, cigarette cases, and other valuable objects, and packed them with the best silver from the dining room, to be deposited in the local bank. It was now well past midnight and a blizzard was blowing outside. Unable to sleep, he began the task of tidying his mother's bedroom and putting everything back where it belonged. Suddenly the front doorbell rang several times, shattering the silence of the big empty house. He went down, convinced that the Gestapo had returned. "I had difficulty in opening the massive twelve-foot-high entrance door against the gusts of wind from the north. A flurry of snow blew into the hall along with a small, sturdy man, Erik Morrill, a local Maribo resident who had known us all for many years. In spite of his wizened arm, he had bicycled the three miles from Maribo, repeatedly falling into snowdrifts, to see if there was anything he could do to help us. No one could have been more welcome at that moment! I thanked him and explained that there was only one thing he could do for us: warn my sister and tell her to try to escape to Sweden as soon as possible. Erik got back on his bicycle and took the first morning train to Copenhagen, a gallant and loyal man."

The next morning Viggo, with the help of his father, locked up the big house. They had two horses harnessed to a sleigh and proceeded to the estate of Jorgen's aunt where, it was decided, Jorgen Wichfeld would remain for the time being. On the way they acquired more cigarettes from a helpful wholesaler and withdrew some money, which later would come in handy with the prison guards. Thus equipped, young Viggo set off for Copenhagen, determined to see his mother

in prison. He learned that she was being held in the West
Prison and that she would not be allowed any visits while
under interrogation. Undeterred, he went to their lawyer's
office and had the secretary type a letter in German on office
stationery, stating that he, Viggo Wichfeld, was hereby authorized to visit his mother on that day. They then stamped
this bogus *laissez-passer* with every available rubber stamp; it
looked impressive and it worked. Viggo described his first
visit:

"After I passed the massive front entrance, guarded by
eight armed German soldiers, I found myself in a dark for-
tress-like outbuilding with another gate ahead, also heavily
guarded. There was a sense of being trapped as I walked
through the next gate, carrying my suitcase, pockets stuffed
with packets of cigarettes. Again I was let through on my
phony pass, with much rattling of locks and keys and clanging
of gates. I felt I was being entombed. Escorted by an armed
German soldier, I came to the center of the complex and was
led into a huge cathedral-like aisle with glass skylights and
tiers of iron balconies on either side. There I was told to wait;
all around me were sounds of locks being turned and distant
footsteps, but not a human voice anywhere. A moment later
my mother was led down the catwalk by an armed guard.
Quick as lightning she ran toward me the moment she reached
the ground floor, so I had time before the guard caught up
with us to whisper that Inkie had gone into hiding and to tell
her the names of all the people arrested. I then gave her the
suitcase, the parcel of food that the farmer's wife had prepared, some ready money, and the cartons of cigarettes. When
the guard started to object, I quickly slipped several packets
into the pocket of his uniform; it had a miraculously quieting
effect."

* * *

Inkie in the meantime was going through agonies of anxiety and indecision. When she received the news of her family's arrest, she realized that she had to go into hiding from
the Gestapo. Jacob had been to her flat in Copenhagen and
it was obvious that they had all been implicated, including
their leader, Flemming Muus, with whom Jacob had been
working for almost a year. A council of war was held in the
dentist's flat, which was Muus's secret safe house. Bobby
Moltke was there—the Germans were now looking for him,
for he too had been betrayed, not by Jacob, but by a captured
secret-radio operator. It was essential for him to leave the
country at once and go to Sweden. Flemming Muus suggested
that Inkie travel with Moltke, but she refused.

Although they did their best to persuade her, she remained adamant. "My mother would be ashamed of me if I
didn't stay," she kept saying. Muus, who secretly wanted to
keep her there, decided she could remain in the country on
one condition, that she "sacrifice her looks." She agreed.
When he met her the next day, he got a shock: the pretty,
blond, curly-haired girl looked like a middle-aged spinster
with masses of unbecoming red curls, horrid bangs, and
glasses that made her appear cross-eyed; she was wearing
clothes in which even her own brother would not have recognized her. Her false identity card was made out in the name
of Kirsten Gade (an amalgam of names picked from the Copenhagen telephone directory).

On the assumption that the last place where the Germans
would be likely to look for her was the small residential hotel
patronized by the women working for the German legation,
Inkie took a room next door to the Secretary of the Reich's

Plenipotentiary, Dr. Best. "We shared a bathroom and a kitchen," she recalls, "and used to exchange pleasantries while making our breakfast, and politely say 'After you' when we met outside the one bathroom, each clutching a kettle of hot water." Work helped to keep her mind off family worries. As Flemming Muus's secretary, she was incredibly busy all the time; she had to be constantly available, ready to turn up at odd hours and odd places to take dictation. She often took down telegrams as they rode in a taxi. Since the formation of the Freedom Council the previous September, in which leaders of the Danish army military intelligence had been working closely with the London-directed SOE agents, she also had to arrange meetings and attend them. She had to put Muus's telegrams to London into code and to decipher incoming messages. It was dangerous and responsible work and she carried it off superbly, winning a place for herself in the history of the Resistance. The mutual admiration and attraction between her and the Boss (as he was known), who several times had asked her to marry him, made her work even more exciting.

Monica's cell was damp and piercingly cold. She lay on her pallet exhausted by the endless interrogations. To weave her way through the minefield of questions required intense concentration, an excellent memory, and alertness on her part. The Germans, convinced that they had a spy of international stature on their hands, put one of their most experienced investigators on the case. His task was made easy by Jacob, who had broken down soon after his arrest and revealed not only the names of Monica's team but the most minute details of the operations. Familiar as he was with the work of the underground, he became directly responsible for the arrests and deaths of over a hundred Danish patriots. His accounts, chillingly accurate, were then put in front of Monica.

How she managed to survive these grueling sessions without ever admitting her involvement or mentioning a single name or event is hard to imagine. She was a delicate woman, no longer young, yet day after day she had to submit to these interviews, a deadly mixture of fact and fiction the Gestapo specialized in. Yet she came through with flying colors; even her interrogator felt defeated when he attempted to bribe her with cigarettes. Monica was a passionate smoker, capable of consuming up to sixty cigarettes a day. The Germans soon discovered her so-called weakness and decided to use it for their own purposes. Ivan, who managed to get an audience with the Gestapo questioner Heinrich Nagel, was told, "Your mother is unwilling to speak, but it might make a difference if we cut off her cigarettes." This they did. After a week of desperate craving Monica was awakened late one night and called in front of her tormentor Nagel. Placing a packet of Chesterfields on the table, he crudely made another attempt to get her talking. "You shall have the whole packet if you reveal your accomplices' names and whereabouts." Monica looked at him with contempt; she flicked her long fingers at the packet, so that it went shooting way underneath the radiator in the room. Nagel, reluctant to part with his cigarettes, had to scramble on his knees in full uniform to pick them up.

On one occasion she was questioned ceaselessly for ten hours. When at about one o'clock in the morning the examining judges were dozing off, Monica got to her feet and announced, "As you seem to be unable to interrogate me properly, I must request you to take me back to my cell. I believe we are wasting each other's time." Only a woman of great intelligence, courage, and unusually steady nerves could have dealt with her jailers the way Monica did. After a month's stay in detention, she was already being called "the queen of the West Prison" by the guards. One particular German orderly was so impressed with her growing stature that he volunteered to smuggle letters from her to her family out of prison, a grave offense had he been caught.

At the back of Monica's mind there dwelt, of course, the ever-present apprehension that one day she might have to submit to torture. The previous autumn, when discussing the possibility of her arrest, she once said to Pastor Marcussen, "I think I could stand almost anything done to me, except perhaps having my fingernails pulled out." Fortunately she was spared; no attempt was ever made to torture her. But prison life presented hardships that, as would any fastidious woman, she must have found particularly repellent. Being locked up in a small, smelly cell was bad enough, but the lack of exercise and fresh air was even worse. She was allowed only one half-hour walk a day, in a bleak triangular courtyard a few feet wide and about thirty yards long. Food consisted of a thin soup, a slice of bread, and ersatz coffee; she was constantly hungry and often thirsty. Worst of all were the sanitary arrangements: "Mrs. Wichfeld and I used to meet in the long galleries of the West Prison, each of us carrying a chamber pot in our hand," recalls Gerner Nielsen of the Sakskøbing asylum. "I thought it grim, but she never lost her sense of humor."

To add to Monica's worries, young Viggo also ended up in the West Prison. Too restless to sit in the country with his father, and encouraged by his success in obtaining permission to visit his mother on a fake pass, he presented himself again at the gate of the prison, but this time he was refused access. Much annoyed, he made his way to the notorious Dagmar House, the Gestapo headquarters in Copenhagen. "After waiting around for some time, I was taken up to see two thug-like men, who were dealing with my mother's case. I asked for a permit to see her, which was instantly refused. I then asked whether I could send her cigarettes, only to be told that she was not allowed to smoke." At this point the twenty-year-old boy lost his cool. Monica's younger son was known for his violent temper, unlike his brother, Ivan, who was languidly self-possessed like Jorgen. Now, outraged, he slammed his fist on the Gestapo officer's desk, demanding that they "treat his mother with decency." In reply he was thrown against the wall, a revolver dug in his ribs, and soon found himself sitting on the floor in the underground garage next to a young Danish prisoner in handcuffs. Soon he was taken to the West Prison, and the iron gates, which had so depressed him on his first visit, clanged shut. He too was "in the bag."

Monica heard of her son's arrest through one of the Danish prisoners, who communicated with her via the prison "telegraph," Morse-code messages relayed from one cell wall to the next. Her cell was unfortunately a long distance from Viggo's, across the main catwalk on the south side of the prison; it made communication difficult. Undaunted, she sent him her Dunhill lighter through a helpful guard. Viggo knew that Dunhill lighters have a secret compartment inside the screw which seals off the fuel; it is designed to hold a spare flint. He promptly unscrewed it and to his joy found a tiny piece of lavatory paper with a message of encouragement from his mother. Contact had been established.

*　*　*

From the very moment of her arrest, it was apparent to
Muus and others in the hierarchy of the underground movement that the case of the *Third Reich vs. Monica Wichfeld*
looked very serious. Although she consistently denied everything and even wore out her interrogators, she was nevertheless confronted with Jacob's encyclopedic memory at every
step. The Gestapo prosecutor believed that she knew far more
than her accuser did. With a view to staging a spectacular
propaganda trial, he was anxious for Monica to admit guilt.
The case dragged on for four months while she was exposed
to additional harassment; neither her husband nor her son
Ivan was allowed to visit her at the West Prison, nor was she
allowed to receive letters. In early March the Resistance leaders decided that an attempt should be made to set Monica
free.

Two former Resistance workers, K. Jessen-Schmidt and
his son Henning, were among the number of people imprisoned by the Gestapo after Jacob's betrayal. They too were
accused of "aiding agents who worked for a foreign power."
Henning, who established contact with Viggo at the Horserød
camp, to which they both had been transferred from the West
Prison, was released in early March for lack of solid evidence.
Back in Copenhagen he secretly met with Inkie and Muus;
he was told that what was urgently needed was a good contact
in the Gestapo headquarters at Dagmar House. Henning was
able to provide this through his friend Claire Schlichting (Mrs.
Buckardt-Hansen), a German cabaret dancer and circus per-
former. German by birth and married to a Dane, Claire
Schlichting was an attractive woman in her thirties, and violently anti-Nazi. She ran a canteen at Dagmar House and
did everything in her power to help the prisoners. Through
her, discreet contact was established with a Gestapo man

called Renner, who was one of the agents in charge of Monica's case. Mercenary by nature, Renner also had a young mistress who was plaguing him to buy her jewelry and a new fur coat.

After careful negotiations through Claire Schlichting, who risked her life by involving herself in the case, Renner agreed, in exchange for the sum of 30,000 kroner (a huge amount of money in those days), to arrange Monica Wichfeld's escape. He was promised that he and his mistress would be given a safe passage to Sweden through the existing underground escape route. On the morning of March 31, Renner was to fetch Monica at the West Prison in a car and a few moments later allow himself to be "overpowered" at the point where the road crosses a railway line over a narrow girder bridge. Jens Peter, a parachutist, and six chosen men were to stage a holdup at the bridge; an ambulance driven by one of the Resistance men, pretending there had been an accident, was to be on the spot, ready to carry Monica to safety with sirens blaring. She was to spend twenty-four hours in a secret hideaway with Inkie in Copenhagen, then be spirited away to Sweden by fast boat. It sounded like a splendidly thought out plan, but it failed. "At 8:45 that morning," recalls Fleming Muus in *The Spark and the Flame*, "Inkie and I stood by a nearby tunnel connecting the two roads. It had been agreed with Jens Peter that he and Hans Johanssen were to meet us there after the action. When my men arrived, there was no need to ask them how it went. One could see on their faces that the news was bad." Renner's car with Monica had failed to turn up. It transpired that Renner, who had received an advance of 10,000 kroner the day before, had got drunk and was discovered lying unconscious in his office, pockets bulg-

ing with notes. He was held for examination and, when in a
condition to talk, explained that he had been bribed and was
"on his way to his superior" to tell about the conspiracy. He
was arrested that evening and sent to the Russian front with
a convict brigade.

In an effort to entrap the organizers of the plot, the Gestapo had sent out a car with a woman dressed like Monica,
but fortunately the parachutists knew Monica well and realized it was not the same person. They gave the prearranged
danger signal and everybody dispersed, making their way
across the bridge in the snow. Monica never learned what
had gone wrong until, while waiting to be interviewed at Dagmar House, her prison companion Jessen-Schmidt offered her
a cigarette, pointing to the lighter, which she recognized as
the one she had sent Viggo in prison with a message. She
then realized something had gone seriously wrong with her
rescue.

Jessen-Schmidt and Claire Schlichting were arrested.
Jorgen and Ivan Wichfeld, neither of whom had any knowledge of the plot, had been attending a wedding reception in
Copenhagen and were arrested at the Hotel d'Angleterre,
dressed in their evening clothes. (They spent a few weeks at
the Horserød camp, but were soon freed.)

Back at the Horserød camp young Viggo was anxiously
awaiting the news which Jessen-Schmidt was to communicate
to him. "It was snowing that day," he recalls, "and our camp
assumed the appearance of a prison in Siberia, hemmed in
by pine trees loaded with snow and surrounded by barbed
wire and guard towers. As the long shuffling queue of prisoners moved forward in their wooden clogs toward the barracks, a man said to me, 'The most extraordinary new

prisoners have just arrived, a father and son. The father is wearing a monocle and they are both in full evening dress.' I felt my legs weaken. The description was all too familiar and I realized that the plot had failed and that my mother's situation was now more hopeless than ever."

A warm friendship developed in prison between Monica and her would-be liberator, Claire Schlichting. This in spite of the fact that they had very few occasions to meet, and had to be content to tap "notes" to each other in Morse code through the wall that separated their adjoining cells. Later they managed to exchange letters, which Claire successfully preserved for Monica's children.

After the unsuccessful attempt to free her, Monica found herself even more isolated. Her husband and two sons were now in prison, her daughter (she fervently hoped) safe in Sweden. Her only contact with the outside world was through the Danish Red Cross. The head of it at the time was Dr. Helmer Røsting; it was said that his sympathies were pro-German, and at first Monica was reluctant to deal with him. After their first meeting, however, Dr. Røsting, dry and humorless functionary though he was, fell under Monica's spell; he genuinely tried to help, established contact with her family, frequently got her the much craved-for cigarettes, and after her sentencing personally intervened with Dr. Best to save her life. With his knowledge of the German mentality and his ability to speak to them, Røsting exerted a beneficial influence in Copenhagen and did much to alleviate conditions not only in the West Prison but in other detention camps in the country. Røsting came to see Monica regularly and she welcomed his visits. She wrote to him after the arrest of her husband and Ivan:

As most of my family are now in prison—they disappear one after another like the ten little nigger boys in the nursery rhyme—and as I would not like my few remaining relatives to end up here, I am sending my fortnightly letter to you [prison regulations allowed her to write once every two weeks], as I don't think there is much danger that *you* will end up in the Dragon's stomach. I would indeed welcome a visit from you and some news of my family. Please give them many messages from me, and tell them that I am in good spirits and will always be so, regardless of what may happen and where I may end up.

Jorgen, who fell ill with pneumonia in the Horserød camp, was released in late April; Ivan too was allowed to go free, but Monica's case dragged on. Ivan obtained another interview with Heinrich Nagel, the Gestapo functionary in charge of his mother's case. "How long is it all going to last?" he asked. With a superior air Nagel answered that he too had come to the conclusion that the case had gone on long enough. He reckoned, he said, on having a decision within two weeks. "Do you think she will be released," asked Ivan, "or will she have to go to Horserød?" Nagel looked at him as one does at an idiot child; he remained silent. "This was the first time that I understood how serious things were for my mother," recalls Ivan. "A terrible thought crossed my mind. Suppose she was to be sent to Germany?"

Viggo, Nielsen, Hovmand, and several others who had been implicated in the case were brought from the detention camps in the country to the West Prison in May. Monica ran into her son by chance one morning on the prison's iron staircase as he was being led out to exercise. To her joy they were able to communicate from then on. This was done with the help of Heinz Neumann, a German guard who was so impressed by Monica's courage that he offered to act as her postman within and outside the prison walls.

On most evenings the West Prison was shaken by distant explosions coming from around Copenhagen. Monica knew this meant acts of sabotage and that someone was probably going to die in reprisal. From early in 1944, when Hitler decreed that terror be used to crush the Resistance, random killings of innocent people followed on the actions of the underground. German police now resorted to measures used in other occupied countries but not previously practiced in Denmark. They raided trains, combed the streets, and rounded up any large gathering, hoping to catch Resistance members who would otherwise be living in secret equipped with false identity papers. More and more groups of parachutists were being sent from England and receivers of air-dropped weapons were being caught; many were tortured. Among the victims was a heroic group centered at the Fiil family inn at Hvidsten in Jutland, the province through which the vital German communication lines with Norway ran. Betrayed by the same Jacob, Marius Fiil and his team were arrested that spring. His young daughter Tulle later joined Monica in prison. The Resistance's response to the terror and to the ever-increasing arrests was to extend their sabotage work. They now had the backing of most of the Danish population, increasingly bitter and openly hostile to the Nazis. The explosions Monica heard took place at the important engineering works around Copenhagen in late April. The Germans, their nerves on edge, expected a cross-Channel invasion and an attack on Norway, and reacted violently. Counterterror was intensified and orders came from Berlin to stamp out sabotage with harsh sentences. Monica's trial took place in this heated atmosphere.

One evening as Monica was knitting in her cell (she had unraveled one of her son's old sweaters and was making a pair of socks for him), she heard the key turn in the lock and a German soldier marched in with a message: She was to be ready the next morning to attend a trial at Dagmar House. So that was it; the endless wait was over.

There were eleven of them marshaled together at the main entrance gate in the light of a perfect May morning. She smiled with pleasure at the familiar faces from Lolland: Gerner Nielsen; Hans Christian Hovmand, who always made her feel cheerful; Wilhelm Grandt, the editor of the Maribo paper; a woman, Else (Pia) Baastrup-Thomsen, who was to become Monica's companion in hardship and a close friend in the forthcoming weeks. Viggo was also led in with five others whom she did not know by sight but whose names, read out in court, were familiar to her from the underground. They were hustled into the main courtyard, where the familiar tarpaulin-covered lorries were waiting. The trucks, very high off the ground, were difficult for a woman in a skirt to get into. As Monica tried to hoist herself up, a young soldier roughly put his hand under her behind and gave her a push. She swung around, slapped his face, then turned back and got onto the lorry unaided. It was all over in a second. The soldier looked stunned, while the convoy of two lorries led by the Gestapo staff car drove onto Copenhagen's main boulevard, over the girder bridge where Monica was to have been freed six weeks earlier.

After months of incarceration, Monica looked with delight at the familiar tree-lined streets in their verdant panoply, felt the warm sun on her face, and watched the groups of pedestrians sauntering along the Istedgade. Life seemed so amazingly normal, as if nothing unusual was happening. She noticed a young man and his girl, arms draped around each other, walking along the pavement, oblivious of the prisoners who passed by them only a yard away. They belonged to a different world, one in which neither Gestapo nor prisons existed, and yet her sacrifice would enable them to lead a carefree existence in postwar years.

On arrival at Dagmar House, the convoy drove down the ramp into the huge underground garage. Armed soldiers stood along the walls, submachine guns at the ready. "We seem to be getting the full treatment," Hans Christian Hovmand whispered to Monica, who was sitting next to him. They were led upstairs under guard.

The setting for the first formal German court-martial in Denmark was a vast, white-painted room, with windows overlooking the town square. In prewar days this had been the boardroom of Kampsax, a Danish company. The room was crowded. Again soldiers with automatic weapons lined the walls. The prisoners were led in to seats in two rows, the second row higher than the first, so that the judges would have a clear view of all the accused. They were a twenty-nine-year-old writer, Georg Quistgaard, a pioneer member of the Danish Resistance involved in arms drops; Arne Lützen-Hansen, a fair young man of medium height who might have passed for a budding executive but was in fact a brilliant radio operator, trained in England; and a thin, pale, boyish-looking man, Carl Jorgen Larsen, the cashier of the Århus Privatbank, who supplied ammunition and funds to saboteurs in Zealand. The three men and Monica occupied the front row. The others sat behind them, with Viggo directly in back of his mother. They faced the prosecutor, a youngish man with the silver SS insignia on his black uniform. Next to him were the two key witnesses—Bent and Jacob, the parachutists—sitting obediently, eyes averted. Jacob looked particularly uncomfortable. The secretary, a high-ranking officer, occupied a place on the right by the window, flanked by two Gestapo Kriminalassistenten. By himself at a small table sat the unprepossessing figure of the so-called defense counsel, young, delicate, nervous, and obviously hating his job, though dutifully anxious to discharge it. Obviously it was to be a show trial.

Everybody stood up as the three judges, all of them wearing their SS military uniforms, entered the room, taking their places under the portrait of Adolf Hitler. Monica was fascinated by the inscription above the Führer's portrait: "The man who cannot defend himself is a coward."

The indictment, "giving aid to the enemy," was read and Monica was the first to be called. She was made to stand all through the examination, but she gave neither the judges nor the prosecution nor the witnesses more than an indifferent glance. The words "denied, but proved by Jacob Jensen's testimony" became a monotonous refrain. "She was marvelous," Gerner Nielsen recalled, "all calm dignity, with just a faint suggestion that the lengthy interrogation was beginning to bore her. When confronted with Jacob she totally ignored him. . . . 'Oh, Jacob!' I wanted to shout, looking at the dismal figure of our accuser, 'why didn't you take that cyanide pill? How will you ever be able to live with yourself from now on?' "

In long diatribes the prosecution was proving that all the accused had deliberately plotted against the Reich; they blackened the character of every prisoner. It all took a long time; the German voices droned on, punctuated by the hourly striking of the town hall clock, its chimes reminiscent of Big Ben's. Monica looked out the window, watching the city pigeons promenading on sun-baked ledges. In the afternoon the court adjourned for two hours; the prisoners were given food and drink and were allowed to smoke. Their mood was cheerful; everyone was relieved to be momentarily out of the dismal prison atmosphere. Monica laughed when she noticed that the napkins produced with the food were imprinted with a jolly message, *Happy Christmas*, now almost six months out of date. "One way to use surplus stock," she remarked to her son.

The next morning was taken up with a lengthy summing-up speech by the prosecutor. He asked for ten years' penal servitude for Monica Wichfeld; slightly less for Georg Quistgaard, Lützen-Hansen, and Carl Larsen; two years for Gerner Nielsen; and recommended that the others be set free, duly warned. It was now the turn of the defense counsel. "Sweat pours down his forehead, he often gets stuck, and his voice trails away," Gerner Nielsen described him in his notes. The counsel's task could not have been easy, as Monica had denied everything. It must have been very difficult both to handle her case and to fulfill the obligatory part of the charade imposed on him by German law. At the end he feebly asked for Monica's sentence to be reduced, "though only slightly, as she has refused to cooperate during the trial." After lunch the judges returned to the improvised courtroom. Again the accused were led in one by one and their particulars carefully recited—name, birthplace, occupation, etc. A prolonged silence ensued, while the presiding judge sternly looked at the two rows of prisoners facing him. In a clear, ringing voice he began to read the sentences, starting from the left of the front row: "Georg Brockhoff Quistgaard, condemned to death; Arne Lützen-Hansen, death; Carl Jorgen Larsen, death; Monica Emily Wichfeld, death."

A gasp greeted the announcement of Monica's sentence. It was the first death verdict pronounced upon a woman in

Denmark for centuries; even during the seventeenth-century witch trials no such sentence had been carried out. It was a solemn and terrible moment, but Monica remained quite unmoved. Conscious of her son sitting behind her, she opened her enameled Tiffany compact, so she could see his reaction in the mirror, smiled at him, and powdered her nose. When the SS officer presiding over the court asked if she had any previous convictions, her rollicking Irish sense of humor prevailed over the tense atmosphere and she burst into free, spontaneous laughter, the kind of mirth with which one greets a really good joke, and replied, "Good heavens, no!" The Germans looked on nonplused as the courtroom was filled with guffaws and the tension was broken. The commanding officer was forced to call for the restoration of order.

After the four death verdicts, hard-labor sentences were pronounced on Gerner Nielsen, Hovmand, and others. (Hovmand's sentence was considerably reduced because of his participation in the 1940 Russo-Finnish War.) Jorgensen, the asylum gardener, and young Viggo were set free for lack of evidence. Pia Baastrup-Thomsen received six years at hard labor.

The three condemned men made stirring patriotic speeches, describing how proud they were of what they had achieved. When her turn came to speak, Monica chose to remain silent. It annoyed one of the judges, who abruptly ordered her to stand up. She rose and looked at the three black-uniformed figures. "Anything else, gentlemen?" she asked, as if ready to dismiss them from her presence. "Yes, you may make an application for mercy, if you wish," said the counsel for the prosecution. "Does that apply to my companions?" "No." "Then it is of no interest." She reached behind her and squeezed her son's hand.

It was over. They were led down to the garage and loaded into the two tarpaulin-covered Black Marias. On the way back to her cell, Monica noticed that one of the condemned men was on the verge of collapse, shedding tears. "Cheer up," she said in her English-accented Danish. "This surely is a unique experience. It can only happen once in a lifetime. We are lucky." The man managed a wan smile. "Thank God!—and bless you for your amazing courage."

Back at the gates of the West Prison she was allowed a brief moment alone with her son Viggo, but by then the strain was beginning to take its toll. She stood rigid, impassive, and silent, while he embraced her for the last time. She then walked slowly back through the gates and heard them clang behind her. That night at 4 a.m., when the prison was unusually quiet, she heard keys being turned in the locks, boots stamping on the cement balcony, voices singing the Danish national anthem. Then distant shots . . . Was it going to be her turn next?

On the evening of the day Monica's death sentence was pronounced, her daughter, Varinka, and Flemming Muus, to whom Inkie had recently become engaged, were staying at a country cottage near Sorø that belonged to their Resistance friends the Hermann Dedichens. Just before going to bed they tuned in to the radio reports from Stockholm for the latest world news. "An important report from Copenhagen," the announcer read. "An official German communiqué has just been issued; it states that on the thirteenth of May 1944, in accordance with military law, the following persons have been sentenced for acting in support of the enemy: Georg Brockhoff Quistgaard, born in Copenhagen, condemned to death." Inkie and Flemming were startled; they had not realized that their friend Georg Quistgaard had already appeared before a court-martial; nor did they yet know about Arne Lützen-Hansen and Carl Larsen. Then to their horror they heard: "Monica Wichfeld, formerly Massy-Beresford, born in London, living at Engestofte, Lolland, condemned to death." There were several other people in the room to whom Inkie was known under her current *nom de guerre*, Miss Hviid. They had no idea there was any connection between her and the woman whose sentence had just shocked them all so much. Inkie was not going to divulge her identity, no matter how much it cost her; nor would she allow herself the slightest expression of grief. She asked for a cigarette, which Flemming Muus lit for her. Moments later she got up from the sofa and said, "Well, I thought we were going to bed early! Good night, everybody." She went up to her bedroom, where she could finally be alone with her thoughts. After the verdicts became public, the office of the Reich's plenipotentiary, Dr. Best, issued a terse communiqué stating that the implementation of the four death sentences was conditional upon the immediate cessation of sabotage actions by the underground. Flemming Muus, deeply affected by Varinka's suffering, offered to cancel all activities for the next few days if it would save Monica's life. But Varinka, who knew her mother's mind, refused. "No, you can't. Our national life is at stake. My mother will take her chance like everyone else. That is what she would wish."

The death sentence of Monica Wichfeld shook the Danes. There was something deeply repulsive to civilized people in the announcement that a woman could be put in front of a firing squad. The ancient Wichfeld family was part of the country's history, and Monica herself was admired and well liked. Furthermore, she was British. In this fifth year of the war Britain was the leader and the inspiration from whom help to the Resistance had flowed. How dare the Germans condemn Monica Wichfeld to death? In the swelling wave of resentment the Danish trade unions threatened a general strike; churchmen throughout the country appealed for prayers; journalists recalled the case of Nurse Edith Cavell, executed by the Germans in Belgium for hiding British prisoners during the First World War. Telegrams and memoranda flew between the British legation in Stockholm and the Foreign Office in London about the fate of "the British-born Monica Wichfeld, now Hitler's hostage." (Monica in fact by marrying a Dane had lost her British nationality and her right to a British passport. Yet the Germans did not consider her Danish and treated her with all the severity reserved for enemy aliens.)

In her cell in the West Prison, daily expecting to be executed, Monica wrote a farewell letter to Claire Schlichting. The letter, which has been preserved by her family, is a moving document, which sums up the unusual personality of this remarkable woman.

My dearest . . . Thank you for everything. I shall *not* forget. It is not that I do not want to see the family, but the *only* thing I cannot bear is to see them suffer. Viggo brought me to the verge of tears when he asked to say goodbye to me the other day. Ivan and the girl are stronger, but my husband and Viggo are weaker. And I *must* remain strong for other people's sake. I have had such luck. —All those I love are free, but there are so many others whose loved ones are either here, or dead, or about to be executed, and it is of *them* that I must think and try to help. I saw it during the courtmartial: one man started to cry and I was afraid that they would all go 'amok'. Something like that is contagious (I have seen it happen in Italy), but when I laughed after receiving my sentence, they all suddenly pulled themselves together and we were all almost cheerful on our way back in the car. I must, whatever it costs me, keep my spirits and my sense of humor to the very end. . . . I have always laughed at fate, always fought against poverty, illness, criticism, etc.

I have always done what I chose to do, even if people found it unsuitable. . . . They had to accept it and take me as I was; and as it was always amusing and exciting in our circle, they finally did not mind. . . . I was born a *Vagabond* and I will always be one. I liked to be alone as a child; sat on a rock by the lake and dreamt of how I would one day make my way out of the narrow world I belonged to and see other countries, get to know a variety of people and live a full life. And I have achieved it. I have lived among kings, grand dukes, artists, writers, diplomats, workmen, spies, Communists, prostitutes, drunkards, and dope addicts, and I have good friends among them all. I have driven in a Rolls to dinner at the Ritz with all my jewels on one night, and I have pawned them the next day to buy medicine for my ailing husband. . . . And I always took it with laughter—so did my family. . . . I have learned that there is no such thing as black or white, only gray. No one is evil through and through. It depends on the upbringing and on the way one reacts to life's difficulties. It is for this reason that I am not afraid to face my God; he knows my sins—and if he has a sense of humor, which I am sure he has, he will just smile at me and let me pass. Say therefore to my children that they must not be unhappy, for I am not. I shall always be near them in their time of trouble. I have asked that my body should be burnt and that the "Blue Danube" be played in the church and that my ashes be strewn somewhere in the Mediterranean, where there is always sunshine and warmth. . . . We do not die, we only sleep a little, to live again as spring follows winter, and when they see my hands or my eyes in their children or hear them say something with my voice, they will no longer grieve.

Dr. Werner Best, the Reich's plenipotentiary, was perplexed. In his luxurious office on Strañdvejeñ he surveyed the pile of situation reports from various parts of the country he had ruled on behalf of the German Foreign Office for the last year and a half. They all told of unrest and of particular indignation at the sentencing to death of a woman. There were even scathing comments in the press of neutral Sweden, a criticism to which Germans were particularly sensitive. Dr. Best was a small, wiry man, whose fast-receding hairline and nervous manner made him appear older than his fifty-odd years. Conscious of Denmark's importance to the economy of the Reich and of its military significance with the impending Allied invasion, he had succeeded in maintaining a tolerable relationship with the Danish administration. The recent rescue of Danish Jews could not have been successfully carried out without Best's turning a blind eye to the escape routes; for this he incurred Himmler's wrath. As the German war fortunes declined and Denmark became progressively pro-Allies, Dr. Best found it more and more difficult to resist Hitler's orders that terror be unleashed against "illegal enemy elements." The death sentences just pronounced by the three Gestapo judges, who took their orders from Berlin, were meant to be a harsh warning to the saboteurs. But why did they have to sentence a woman? Unlike Himmler, whom he hated, Werner Best believed terror to be counterproductive. He knew it was in his power to rescind at least one of the sentences.

When Helmer Røsting, the director of the Danish Red Cross, urgently asked for an audience, Dr. Best received him at once. Røsting was eloquent and persuasive. He warned of the "explosive consequences" the execution of Mrs. Wichfeld would have in Denmark and abroad. It might perhaps be legally justified, he argued, but it would be seen as an inhumane act for which he, Dr. Best, would personally be blamed after the war was over. (Both men by now believed that Germany would be vanquished.) He reminded the general of the famous case of Nurse Cavell, and drew his attention to the fact that Monica was the sister of a British brigadier general. He also told him of the deep outrage expressed by the Danish Queen Alexandrine,* herself a Mecklenburg-Schwerin, at this latest manifestation of her nation's inhumanity toward an English-born woman.

Best had felt all along that it was not worth the price to have Monica executed; he would reprieve her. But she must first file a petition for clemency. Røsting returned to the West Prison that evening with what he thought was excellent news. But Monica's first question was "And what about the others?" On hearing they would not be included in the pardon, she shook her head sadly. "What's the use, then? Better to leave things as they are," she told Røsting. It was Claire Schlichting who finally persuaded Monica to file the requested application for mercy. "I beseeched her," she recalled, "to do it for the sake of her family and for Denmark, where she would be needed after the war. But it was only after a long period of reflection, when I had almost lost hope, that she agreed to do it. Even then, though writing paper was available, she used a rough bit of something that looked like the prison toilet paper on which to compose a short, dignified defense of her case. A few days later her reprieve was announced in an official news bulletin, issued by General Dr. Best's office and distributed to all the Danish newspapers and the radio: 'The

---

*The queen, who was a friend of Monica's mother, had a chair sent to Monica at the West Prison. It was returned to the palace by a German guard with a note: "*Das ist kein Hotel.*" (This is not a hotel.)

penalty of death pronounced upon Monica Emily Wichfeld has mercifully been altered to life imprisonment.' "

All Denmark rejoiced. Huge placards carrying the news appeared on Copenhagen's street corners; newsboys ran down the tree-lined avenues shouting, "Mrs. Wichfeld reprieved"; Danish radio issued special bulletins. With the war entering its final stage, life imprisonment could not mean what it said. Tension was momentarily relaxed, though it soon started to build up again after Monica's three colleagues were executed a few days later.

Ivan Wichfeld now went to see Dr. Best in an attempt to prevent the sentence being served in a German prison. He pleaded that in view of his mother's state of health and her age, it would be tantamount to the death penalty. But he met with implacable resistance; Dr. Best stated that he had shown great mercy, which he hoped was duly appreciated by the family and the country. There was nothing more he could do; justice had to take its course. He assured Ivan, however, that conditions in German prisons were "excellent—much better than in Denmark, and medical personnel are available whenever needed." "All this," Ivan recalls, "was said with a straight face and intense seriousness." Governor Best had played a skillful propaganda game and bought time for himself by appearing magnanimous, but Monica's intuition had been right. The reprieve was a hollow gesture—it only prolonged her life for a few months, but during that time she would have to endure intense suffering: there were to be moments when she wished she *had* died in front of the firing squad.

At four o'clock on the morning of June 2, 1944, four days before D-day, when the Allied forces launched their assault on Hitler's Europe, a prison warden opened the door of Cell

No. 265 in the West Prison and informed Monica Wichfeld that she was to "leave *now*." She was prepared. Dressed in her Harris-tweed costume, her shoes well polished, she concealed in one of her pockets a small orchid that Direktør Røsting had brought her. Her nails were well manicured and on her wrist was her Cartier watch; she turned around and looked for the last time at the cell, with its gray-painted walls and hard bed, which had been her refuge for the last four months. She straightened up and walked along the iron bridge to the precipitous stairway, while a guard behind her carried her two suitcases. "She walked like a queen," recalls Claire Schlichting, who was allowed to say goodbye. "Her carriage was proud and elegant, grief was out of the question, only pride in the knowledge that she had done what was right. I saw a German soldier bow and kiss her hand and heard him murmur, 'I admire you.' She departed as if she were on her way from a great international hotel to the railway station, leaving a hushed prison behind her."

Nine

Prisoner in Germany

THE CANVAS-COVERED German troop carrier drove into the courtyard of the West Prison to collect the three Danish women sentenced to penal servitude in Germany—Monica Wichfeld, Else (Pia) Baastrup-Thomsen, and Greta Jensen, a young girl from Ålborg in Jutland, who like Pia had been given six years for sheltering a parachutist. To guard them the military police had detailed six heavily armed soldiers, two submachine guns, and two army motorcycles, each carrying two more armed men. As the military vehicle and its escort drove out of the huge iron gates, a Danish prison officer raised his cap in a respectful salute to the women. They turned toward the harbor, where two more guards were collected (it was learned that the Germans had been afraid of a Resistance ambush to free Monica), past the statue of the Copenhagen Little Mermaid glittering in the June sunshine. Soon they were driving along the Køge highway toward the harbor of Gedser, at the southernmost tip of the island of Falster. All around them spread the fields and rich pastures of Zealand, neat farms, thatched cottages, and cows grazing in the luscious green meadows; the yellow-green fields of corn, scattered with poppies, looked almost ready for harvest. As they came to the point where the road runs close to the sea for several miles in a perfectly straight stretch of highway, Monica, who until then appeared plunged in thought, turned her head and looked out the window with a wistful expression. This was the road along which she and Kurt used to race their cars in years past—he in his yellow Hudson, she in her old white convertible. In those days she was an avid reader of Michael Arlen's *The Green Hat* and liked to think of herself as Iris March, so much in love, driving her car recklessly.

"All three of us began our journey in good spirits," recalls Pia in her memoir. "We were perhaps somewhat worried at the thought of leaving Denmark, but after several months in the West Prison I, at least, looked forward to something else. Our luggage was packed with warm clothes, cigarettes, sweets, medicines, everything kind relatives had provided. Little did we know that many of these precious commodities would be taken away from us long before we got to our final destination. Both Grete and I, who were younger, felt slightly in awe of Mrs. Wichfeld, an older woman, still beautiful, with particularly wonderful eyes. Her hair was blue-black with whitish streaks at the temples. While in prison I had always admired her proud carriage, and how she always greeted us when we met in such a charming and endearing way. . . . We all three kept our spirits up during the drive down over Zealand; talking together eagerly, eating and smoking, for we had been told by the soldiers that no smoking would be permitted in Germany. I noticed that after we crossed the bridge into Falster and drove past the island of Lolland, Mrs. Wichfeld's eyes filled with tears. But then a moment later she smiled."

The main road into Gedser was blocked by a convoy that

day, and they took a roundabout way via Lolland. It brought them within sight of Maribo Lake, the beech woods and lime trees in the distance. She could not quite see Engestofte, but as they turned, Rosenlund, Kurt's farmhouse, came into view, and beyond it loomed Hardenberg Castle. She thought of Hardenberg and its host—the utmost in refined luxury; then she looked at the troop carrier, the soldiers, the machine guns—and she laughed.

They came to the Gedser ferry about noon. It was still the same spick-and-span Danish harbor where the Wichfelds had arrived from Italy less than three years before—a lifetime ago. This being Friday, the little port was bustling with fishing boats discharging catches. On hearing that the ferry arriving from Germany would be two and a half hours late, the German guards briskly ordered Monica and her companions into the little waiting room, out of sight of the other passengers and local people. While the six guards, now in a much more relaxed mood, settled down to consume beer and sausages, Monica managed to attract the attention of a Danish woman polishing the windows at her end. The woman realized who Monica was, and cautiously maneuvered near to her chair so that Monica was able to whisper a message to be transmitted to Engestofte. That was how her husband and Viggo learned that she had left Denmark.

As the three women stepped onto the ferry, pushed unceremoniously ahead with the butts of the soldiers' rifles, a great shout of encouragement arose from their fellow Danes, who had hurriedly assembled on the quay as the news of the prisoners' departure spread through town. "Give my love to Denmark," said Monica to a group of burly young fishermen as she passed them on the way to the gangplank. Her companions waved to the crowd. Warnemünde was a mass of ruins, but the ferry terminal, provisionally reconstructed, kept going. As in the rerun of an old movie, as she said in her letters, Monica relived the dramatic night they had spent there. Now it was hard to identify any of the landmarks. War- nemünde, like all German towns in the vicinity, looked almost like a crater-studded landscape on the moon.

Their destination was the women's prison in Kiel, a few hours west on the train. Pushed into an empty third-class carriage that their guards commandeered at gunpoint, Mon- ica looked out of the window at the flat, fertile, North German plain, crisscrossed by rivers. The train inched slowly along a track which had been frequently bombed and had only re- cently been repaired. They passed the old Hanseatic city of Lübeck, once the jewel of the land of Oldenburg, and followed the Elbe to Kiel, the chief naval port of Germany on the Baltic, in the province of Schleswig-Holstein, which only seventy years before had belonged to Denmark. Monica recalled being told at Engestofte of how the Danish-born Alexandra, wife of Edward VII, had "hated the Kaiser, and refused to talk to him at the funeral of her husband in London, because he had dared to take away Schleswig-Holstein from her coun- try." It was obvious, looking out the windows of the train, that Kiel with its magnificent harbor had been the object of heavy bombardment by Allied planes. As the faint outline of the old town of Kiel and the harbor became visible in the distance, their train suddenly ground to a stop in the midst of what appeared to be a marshy wasteland. An air raid alert had just been sounded. There was controlled panic among the pas- sengers; even the guards in Monica's compartment became silent and appeared to have lost their truculence. Air attacks on trains make the occupants feel totally exposed, trapped and helpless. A number of civilian passengers got out, looking for ditches and trying to scatter in the marshy meadows. From their heavily guarded compartment Monica and her companions could hear the bombs falling on the great city; they saw smoke and a fiery glow. Wave after wave of heavy bombers came and went, discharging their deadly cargo. Some three hours later the all-clear sounded. The train started off again, crawling along, circling the town, until it pulled into the Kiel Anhalter Bahnhof, its huge domed roof a skeleton of girders against the sky. It was midnight when they finally disembarked. The guards accompanied them to the prison.

Pia's description: "We were told to run across the courtyard, and fast, because the fierce Alsatian guard dog was loose. The day before he had apparently savaged a man to death. We were then confronted by a very bad-tempered German woman wardress, the first in a long series of similar monsters we were to become acquainted with. She instantly separated us, and after hurling abuse at each one in turn for arriving late, as if we had been responsible for the air raid, she locked us up in separate cells. They were tiny, whitewashed, and with nothing in them except a bunk and a white china pot, which we later learned to call by its German name, the *Kübel*. At that time, unlike Denmark, there were no lavatories in German prisons. Having been up for almost twenty-four hours I fell on the bed and went to sleep."

They did not sleep very long. At 4:30 the next morning Monica and her companions were awakened. After a breakfast of coffee made out of sugar beets and a single slice of black rye bread, they were taken to a room on the other side of the courtyard, where they were told to strip. Their own clothes were packed and taken away; in return they were given some "weird and hideous-looking garments": wooden clogs, gray stockings, bloomers with a patch at the back, and dismal black dresses with yellow armbands, sign of prisoner status. With German efficiency they were handed receipts for their belongings and were told that Kiel was to be only a temporary stopping place; everything would be returned to them when they left. That night, as the prison was filling up, all three were put together in one cell. "Mrs. Wichfeld had been cunning enough to snatch one of her own packets of cigarettes and matches and a small bar of chocolate from her suitcase while the metamorphosis was taking place," recalled Pia. "That evening, as we lay on our mattresses on the floor, we had quite a nice time—we talked and laughed, ate the pieces of chocolate, smoked, and dreamed of when we would get home again."

That was Pia's interpretation of their mood. She and Greta were about half Monica's age, strong, robust, and with a countrified background. Their sentences were comparatively light—they had every reason to hope for a speedy release. They joked at their "hideous disguise," but for Monica, to be separated from her own clothes and forced to don a prisoner's uniform meant losing her identity. Her pride and her aesthetic sense were insulted. Yet she felt it was her responsibility to keep up the morale of her two young cellmates, and she succeeded.

To add to her miseries she was suffering from a vicious toothache. In January, just before her arrest, she had traveled to Copenhagen to see her dentist; he had put in a temporary filling which contained arsenic, warning her that it should be removed after a few weeks when it would stop being effective, otherwise the pain would return. While Monica was in the West Prison, her friend Clara Hasselbach, who had heard about the problem from Monica's worried dentist, bravely went to the dreaded Dagmar House to try to arrange for their dentist to see Monica in prison. "A toothache? Just the thing to make her open her mouth," the Gestapo official replied to Clara's entreaties. "Besides," he said, "we have excellent dentists in our prisons." Permission was thus bluntly refused, and soon after, Monica left for Germany with a toothache. She had to endure the acute pain for three weeks until a humane warden agreed to take her to the hospital after they arrived at Cottbus.

It was in Kiel, on the fifth day of their stay, that they heard about the Normandy landings. They were summoned to the changing room, in preparation for travel; their clothes were returned to them, together with a German-issue toothbrush, a comb, and a piece of soap, which contained about 5 percent fat. The rest of their luggage was to be forwarded to Cottbus, their final destination. (When the luggage finally caught up with them, they discovered that all the food and cigarettes so lovingly packed for them by relatives in Denmark had disappeared.) The young blond German guard in charge of the clothes depot at the Kiel prison came from Schleswig-Holstein. While filling in the required forms, he lifted his pen for a moment, looked around, and whispered, "The attack on Europe has begun, they came on land yesterday." He then went on with his work. So here it was—the most wonderful news in the world—the final stage of this interminable war, they hoped.

That night they were taken to the Kiel station to await departure for Hamburg. The station and the surrounding areas were a scene of frantic activity, crammed with soldiers in full combat gear boarding transports that left for the Western Front every two hours. It was a warm starry night. Monica sat on her suitcase near a disused bit of railway track, thankful that no air-raid warning had been sounded; surely all the planes would be needed to support the landings in France. Hours passed, but the train to Hamburg failed to materialize, much to the annoyance of her guards. It did not upset her; she sat there motionless, her thoughts with the Allied troops pouring onto the beaches of France.

From the distance could be heard the rhythmic footsteps of an approaching platoon and a song. It came floating to her from among the devastation, a chorus of young, strong, marching males singing the haunting ballad "Lilli Marlene," capturing the poignant feel of a fighting man's passing romance and his fugitive lovemaking before going off into battle. "Lilli Marlene" was the one wartime melody which had become a favorite of both sides; it was immortalized by Marlene Dietrich:

> *Outside the barracks, by the corner light,*
> *I'll always stand and wait for you at night.*
> *We'll create a world for two. I'll wait for you*
> *The whole night through,*
> *For you, Lilli Marlene, for you, Lilli Marlene.*

The marching soldiers were now nearing the station. One could easily distinguish the words and see that their faces were very young.

> *When we are marching in the mud and cold,*
> *And when my pack seems more than I can hold,*
> *My love for you renews my might.*
> *I'm warm again, my pack is light,*
> *It's you, Lilli Marlene, it's you, Lilli Marlene.*

The three women looked at each other. "Poor devils," said Monica, "and their lives are only beginning." At this moment the train for Hamburg pulled into the station. Amid shouts of *"Einsteigen!"* they were led through the crowds to a special carriage with cells. This was a new experience. Until now they had traveled, flanked by their guards, in ordinary third-class compartments on an ordinary civilian train. But here each railway wagon was divided into a mass of small rooms down both sides of a central passage. Each tiny room was designed for two people, but they found themselves squeezed in with three others. Two sat on a wooden bench, while the remaining four had to stand upright, tightly pressed against each other, swaying with the motion of the train. There was a window in the cell, but the weave of the metal grating was so dense that it was impossible to see out. Monica had managed to smuggle a pencil; they took turns writing their names and messages on the walls in Danish for others who might be coming this way. By coincidence Tulle Fiil was put in the same train cell four months later and read them. As she recalled when she joined them at Cottbus, "That was when I realized I was not alone any longer."

Hamburg is about sixty miles from Kiel, but the journey in the cell wagon took the whole night over tracks which had been badly disrupted. They emerged into the devastated Hamburg station in the radiant sunshine of a perfect June morning. While one of the guards went off to get transport, Monica looked with amazement at the ruins of the once proud city, the jewel of the Hanseatic League, which for centuries had governed itself independently of its Prussian neighbor. (Since the preceding year, over ten thousand tons of bombs had been dropped on the city, leaving over a million people homeless and killing an estimated 50,000 people, more than died in the United Kingdom from bombing.) On the journey to prison she saw the proud mansions of the city's merchants laid waste around the spectacular Alster lakes, and acres of infinite desolation, punctuated by many broken church spires, still visible against the watery blue northern sky.

On arrival at the prison, which was in the center of town and had been badly bombed the week before, they were put in a large cell with six beds, a lavatory, and running water; this was a vast improvement on Kiel. The inmates of the cell just before their arrival had been prostitutes, picked off the streets, with various forms of venereal disease. The three women lay down fully dressed and fell asleep, only to be roused a few hours later and ordered down to a cellar, as an air-raid warning had just been sounded.

After a week in the Hamburg jail Monica, Pia, and Grete were again locked up in a cell wagon on a train and dispatched to Hannover. "This was the worst of the lot," recalls Pia Baas-trup-Thomsen. "We had to live in a cellar with about a hundred other prisoners. There were beds for only twenty people and they were all occupied by the German 'ladies of the night.' The rest of us foreigners—French, Belgians, Russians, and Danes—had to lie on the floor. Mrs. Wichfeld took all this, as she did all physical and mental hardships, with admirable good humor and optimism, which impressed and inspired us. We were almost ashamed to complain. After all, she was a generation older and had been used to a much more comfortable life than we had; and she had given it all up for Denmark, her adopted country, not even her own."

In Leipzig, where the prison had been destroyed by bombs, they were put in a barracks, sharing a hall with more than a hundred prisoners. There were several large open windows, giving out onto a large leafy courtyard through which they could get whiffs of much-needed fresh air. Monica, with Pia's help, managed to maneuver near a window at the far end and spent the night sitting on the floor, looking at the clear, starry Saxon sky. Two days later, having traveled for over three weeks since leaving Denmark, they finally reached their destination—the penal servitude prison at Cottbus, a town about a hundred miles northeast of Dresden, where they were to remain incarcerated for the next six months.

While Monica and her companions were making their painful progress to the East, mounting unrest in Denmark was gradually working up to an explosion. The death sentence passed on Monica Wichfeld, her subsequent reprieve under pressure, followed by her deportation for penal servitude in Germany, had provoked widespread fury, as did the execution of her associates Quistgaard, Lützen-Hansen, and Larsen. There is no doubt that Monica would have been executed with the others, but the Germans feared her death would precipitate an uprising, forcing them to divert troops to Denmark. The uprising took place anyway, six weeks later, but in the meantime the terror spread. In May there were five more executions, and in the first week of June, thirteen railway workers in Jutland were condemned to death. In response, the Resistance stepped up their attacks on factories working for the German war effort and almost completely disrupted rail communications in Jutland, essential for German troop movements to and from Norway. News of the Normandy landings was greeted with universal joy and enthusiasm, and so was Eisenhower's message to the occupied countries: "The hour of liberation is near." After the largest munitions-manufacturing plant was blown up in the Copenhagen harbor by underground workers in full daylight, the Germans went on a rampage. Overruled by Berlin and pressed by General von Hanneken, Reich's plenipotentiary Best unleashed German terror gangs in the capital.

On Sunday, June 25, the Tivoli pleasure gardens, beloved by the inhabitants of Copenhagen, were pillaged and burned to the ground "to punish the population." At the same time a curfew was proclaimed from 8 p.m. to 5 a.m. Anyone seen outside between those hours was to be shot. In Denmark's northern latitudes the sun does not set in the summer until after 11 p.m. This was June, it was hot, and people refused to obey and stay indoors. Motorized German patrols were powerless in the face of jeering, aggressive crowds. No sooner was one street cleared with the help of gunshots than the people were back again; they lit bonfires and erected barricades. Tension was rising to the boiling point.

The execution of the heroic Marius Fiil, his son, his son-in-law, and his team turned out to be the final straw. In one day the tiny village of Hvidsten in Jutland was decimated. Fathers, brothers, husbands, sons were killed. Marius's two daughters were deported to Germany. (Gerda, the younger, was released, while Tulle joined Monica in Cottbus.) The next morning Copenhagen erupted and a general strike was declared. As the public stopped the trams in the streets, the conductors and tram drivers joined the strikers. Shortly thereafter the workers running the underground and the telephone operators joined up. Road transport became totally paralyzed. When news of the strike spread through the city, tens of thousands of workers left their factories, offices, and shops, pouring out into the streets. No one paid any attention to the curfew; the people had had enough. Copenhagen was in open revolt; everywhere primitive barricades were being built, designed to impede German traffic; they flew Danish, British, and often Russian flags. As the situation became more serious, troops were moved into Copenhagen from all over Denmark, preparing to crush the uprising by tanks and machine guns.

Inkie, who had married Flemming Muus on June 8, continued with her dangerous work. They had moved to a small safe house just outside Copenhagen from which they traveled to town every day. Flemming was now a member of the Freedom Council, the secret governing body of Denmark. The Germans had set a price of one million kroner on his head, but he brilliantly managed to cover his tracks in spite of several narrow escapes. Inkie described the dramatic events of the strike: "Trains, trams, telephones, shops, everything has stopped working. The roads are thick with people on bicycles leaving the city. The weather is perfect and everyone enjoys the thought of an unexpected holiday at the same time as thwarting the Germans. Our policeman friend came to fetch us, for there were no other means of transport, and we crept around corners in his car always on the lookout for trouble. We saw one man shot by a patrol for no apparent reason." Then she added: "The strike lasted four days and it was the most exciting experience I have ever had; at one point the Germans turned off the water, gas, and light. The water was the worst, but people helped each other and emptied the boilers in the cellars. Flemming shaved one morning in half a bottle of soda and I had the other half to wash in. At night the Germans patrolled the streets on foot or in tanks, firing in every direction. I lay on my tummy on the balcony and watched them pass. The Freedom Council held a meeting, at which I was present, and composed a declaration on the people's behalf, saying that if the curfew was abolished and the hated Danish SS bands removed from Copenhagen, the strike would end. . . . I still have the original of this declaration; I kept it after typing it out ready for the underground press."

The Freedom Council's tough stance impressed Best; he charged G. F. Duckwitz, his assistant, who had helped with the escape of the Jews and was known for his sympathy with the Danes, to negotiate. After two days of talks the Germans bowed to the council's demands, withdrew the troops from the capital, restored the utilities, and rescinded the curfew. "The battle is won," the Freedom Council proclaimed, urging everyone to resume work. A total catastrophe was averted, but the strike took its toll: over one hundred people were killed in the streets and six hundred wounded. "How Mummy would have enjoyed being in Copenhagen all this week," Viggo remarked to his brother, Ivan, as they walked in the woods at Engestofte. Both brothers and their father were haunted by the thought of Monica languishing in a German jail. They were totally without news. The Red Cross was their only channel, but even Dr. Røsting, Monica's foremost admirer, found it impossible to establish speedy lines of communication with the Cottbus prisoners' camp. It was late November before Monica's first letter finally reached Engestofte.

The strain of waiting for news was somewhat easier for Inkie, immersed in her new marriage and the dangerous, all-consuming work which claimed all her concentration and emotional resources. Ivan, too, was busy coping with his lovely, impractical wife, but for Jorgen Wichfeld and young Viggo it became the most terrible of summers. Monica's presence permeated every corner of the lovely old house on the lake: they half expected to come upon her arranging flowers on the terrace, reading in her favorite Victorian wing chair in the red sitting room, or walking in the park with the dogs. Jorgen ordered that the door to her bedroom remain shut; the room must not be disturbed in her absence. All through that cruelly beautiful summer and autumn, Engestofte figuratively held its breath, awaiting Monica's return.

In England a frail old lady, bowed with worry, wrote to the Foreign Office in London asking for news of her daughter. She had been told that the British legation in neutral Sweden was following Monica's case. (Most of what was happening in Denmark was known to the well-organized Danes in Stockholm.) Alice Massy-Beresford had already lost a son in World War I; her eldest son, Brigadier Tim, was a prisoner of the Japanese, and her daughter was imprisoned in Germany. She dreaded to think of the conditions her beautiful Monica must be living in.

Dear Mr. Butler [she wrote from Gloucestershire on August 18, 1944, to the head of the northern department of the Foreign Office], You were so kind to me, offering your help at the time when my daughter Monica Wichfeld was sentenced to death, that I venture to appeal to you again. I have heard, through my Danish son-in-law's relations at the Danish legation in Washington, that she might have been moved to Germany. With Himmler in supreme command there, I am more anxious about her than I have ever been. If you are able to get news through any of your sources of information as to where she is and how she is being treated, I shall be more than grateful. I am sorry to trouble you!

Yours sincerely,

Alice Massy Beresford

[From FO 371–43066, Public Records Office, London]

It appears from contemporary records that a bureaucratic wrangle ensued between the Northern Department and the British Legation chancery in Sweden about the "competence" of the department to inquire about Monica's whereabouts. After Stockholm passed on information obtained through SOE channels—to the effect that Monica was now in a prison in Kiel and about to be transferred farther east—the Foreign Office wrote again:

From the Northern Department to the Chancery in Stockholm

September 9th, 1944

Dear Chancery,

I remind you that we are *only* concerned with British civilian internees in enemy hands, but *not* aliens, whose nationality of origin might have been British. Mrs. Wichfeld by marrying a Dane has forfeited her British nationality; she really is not our concern any more. I realize that she is a daughter of prominent British parents and that she has many friends in this country, who have been inquiring about her, but it is not really within our competence to deal with this case.

(signed) Garrett

Northern Department

When this was passed on to Monica's mother, she thereafter dealt through the Red Cross.

One evening, back in the days of Campo dei Fiori in Rapallo, a family discussion had taken place on the meaning and purpose of life. Monica, recently returned from Paris for the summer, stretched on the flowered divan on the terrace, inserted a cigarette in her favorite long jade holder, and declared: "To me life has always seemed to be like a stage. For you never know when you will suddenly get caught in the spotlight. It may be for only an instant, but at that moment you will be the focus of attention. Your entire life might have been a preparation, a rehearsal for this one brief moment in the limelight. It could reveal comedy or tragedy, heroism or cowardice, but that will be *your* moment—no one else's." For Monica such a moment was her capture by the Nazis. Caught in the full glare of history, she was able to play her role with dignity and composure, even greatness. It would undoubtedly have been easier had she been allowed to exit from life at that moment, but Monica's mission on earth was not yet over: she was meant to impart her strength and bring comfort to others during the months spent in the German prison. Unobserved by the world at war, she called upon her great intelligence and experience to sustain and relieve the appalling daily lot of her fellow prisoners. She came to be regarded in prison as the very personification of courage.

"Our cell in Cottbus became a mini-university," Pia Baastrup-Thomsen recalled. "We learned English, Italian, and French history, studied the rise of Mussolini and of Hitler, followed in the footsteps of Mrs. Wichfeld's travels from Ireland and Scotland to England and Italy across France. She managed to structure our day so that the grim external circumstances faded into the background." Their "abode" consisted of a wooden two-tiered bed and an iron bedstead that could be folded up against the wall. There was a table, two wooden benches, and the inevitable *Kübel*, or chamber pot, which could be emptied only once a day. The little water they were given was hardly enough to supply drink and still leave enough to wash in, let alone to clean their floor and launder clothes; yet by some cleverly efficient scheming, they managed to preserve basic standards of hygiene.

To protect her young companions from the sinister women wardens—the *Wachtmeisterin*—Monica devised a daily quota of completion for the work they were assigned to in their cell. At first they were given small pieces of gauze and ordered to make wads or plugs out of them—1,200 a day, preferably 1,500, they were told. When it became obvious that such quotas could not be met, Monica managed to have them cut down. Then they were ordered to unravel miles of string, which had been used for binding bales of hay. This went fast but "we always managed to leave a couple of knots in each batch, hoping they would wreck the harvesting machine." Then corn leaves were issued, which had to be plaited into mats and floor coverings. Monica was particularly skilled at this work; she even made a few souvenirs for her cellmates like belts, slippers, and small wastebaskets. In the evening after a meal consisting of a watery soup and one piece of black bread, tasting of sawdust, "it always took a long time to work out bearable sleeping arrangements, to avoid insect bites and the bedbugs which flourished in the wooden crevices of the cells," noted Pia. "We then lay down and reviewed what Mrs. Wichfeld had taught us during the day; sometimes she would put us through a kind of quiz—to see how much we remembered. She was unfailingly even-tempered, though we knew that she really suffered from being deprived of tobacco."

In late August two Belgian women were unexpectedly added to their already overcrowded cell. Cottbus was filling up; there were now over two thousand prisoners, most of them foreigners—French, Belgian, Polish, and Dutch women and about two hundred Germans—in for "anti-Nazi crimes." They were kept in a separate wing and were rarely allowed in the exercise yard. To guard this vast collection of women

there was a strong detachment of soldiers and an entire platoon of women wardens.

Gertrude Sauchel was the head, the *Direktorin*, a trim,
vigorous woman in her late forties, brown braids neatly twisted
around her head, small brooch, forest-green skirt, sensible
shoes. She lived in a house on the grounds with her husband
and three children. Protective of her family, she could at the
same time display extraordinary cruelty. She ran her prison
with a hand of iron, barked orders in curt, gruff sentences,
terrified the inmates, and was alternately admired and detested by her staff. Yet her face with its pale blue eyes and
rosy cheeks registered satisfaction at a life well lived and a
job worthy of her talents.

Monica and her companions soon took the measure of
the half dozen wardresses who supervised the wing they were
in. At first glance they looked deceptively mild, with their neat
blond hairdos and athletic squat figures beginning to run to
fat. Their strident voices shouting "Heil Hitler!" echoed down
the endless prison corridors. Pragmatic bureaucrats like their
boss, they radiated satisfaction with their careers under the
stirring motto "We German women love our Führer." Having
sworn allegiance to the Nazi creed, they went about their
business, no matter how evil, fortified by a curious morality.
Cottbus was not a concentration camp and Frau Sauchel and
her assistants did not have to emulate the excesses of the
ignoble Irma Griese, "the Bitch of Auschwitz," nor were they
encouraged to carry whips on their daily rounds like Buch-
enwald's Ilse Koch. Yet they practiced, or naturally felt, utter
indifference to human suffering. In spite of the heroic resistance of many, who paid dearly for going against the tide, the
documentary records show that about eight million German
women enrolled in Nazi organizations of all kinds throughout

the war. Very few women became part of the Nazi hierarchy and the Nazi regime was basically anti-feminist, yet women played a vital role in the consolidation of Hitler's rule. In spite of the reams written on the Nazi era, it still remains a mystery how these mothers, constantly exhorted to produce more and more children for the Reich, supported a regime responsible for so much death. Yet they flocked in droves to support their Führer, indifferent to the horrors the Nazis perpetrated, until the final catastrophe engulfed them all.

The arrival of the two Belgian women brought news and excitement into Monica's cell. Maria Boucher and her sister had been imprisoned at Halle, where they had managed to read a few newspapers and talk to recent Allied prisoners. They were able to share the latest news from the outside world: the Allied drive through France toward Paris, the July 20 attempt on Hitler's life, the Russian advance to the Vistula. Monica drew a map on a piece of paper which they carefully hid under the mattress. How long would it take the Allies to get to Berlin? Would they, the prisoners, be able to survive until then? "Monica never let us doubt it for a moment," recalled Pia, but they all knew that "in Cottbus one's fate was in the hands of the wardresses."

Each morning they were awakened at 4:30 and had to start work immediately; otherwise it would have been impossible to fulfill the required work quota. (After working on floor mats, they were ordered to repair army belts.) They took turns sitting by the window, sewing, so that they could keep an eye on the groups taking their exercise in the morning. "The first shift at 6 a.m. usually consisted of Frenchwomen; many of them were young, even beautiful," remembered Maria Boucher. "One could see that they took trouble not to deteriorate. Those who had not been shorn still had lovely hair; most of them still seemed unbowed. Passing the wardens on duty, they did not give them a glance but eagerly talked among themselves; the wardresses raged at their impertinence, but couldn't do anything, as neither party spoke the other's language. But they found victims for their frustration. When one beautiful black-haired girl spread out her shapeless prison uniform and tried to skip farther up the line to get some much needed exercise, she was brutally dragged out of the line and taken away to a solitary-confinement cell in the basement. I heard the wardress say that she would remain there on bread and water for six weeks. . . . It was certain to undermine even the most robust constitution."

Due to a clever stratagem, the gallant, intractable French girls were able to obtain the latest news from French prisoners of war who worked in the fields outside the confines of the women's prison and surreptitiously listened to the BBC. Now and then taking advantage of a guard's momentary absence, one of them would climb a tree near the wall and in rapid French shout *les dernières nouvelles*, the latest news. On the evening of August 25 the entire French contingent went mad. The BBC had reported that Paris was liberated. General Leclerc's army was marching up the Champs-Elysées, the Germans were fleeing. The news spread like wildfire through the prison. The enraged wardresses found it difficult to control the excitement. "Their furious orders of *Halt's Maul* [Shut up!] echoed through the courtyards, but the effect was merely comic," recounted one of the prisoners. Monica, sitting by the window late that night, realized that something important had happened. The ill-famed solitary cells lay under her window and it was from there that she heard a French voice whispering: "*Camarade Danemark, Paris est libéré. Vive la France!*

Vive le Danemark!" It was the girl with the beautiful black hair, confined to the damp basement, who was happily imparting the news.

In early September the air raids began to get closer to Cottbus. Every day, around one o'clock in the afternoon, there was an air-raid warning; one could hear the thud of the exploding bombs in the distance. The wardresses, unaccustomed to air raids, displayed a certain amount of nervousness; special uniforms and matching helmets were issued, and the wardens grimly took up their posts by the fire escapes as soon as the alarm sounded. "It was obvious," wrote Pia, "that they would not for a moment think of unlocking our cells, but would only try to save their own skins. Though we usually had to wait a long time for our evening soup after such an alarm, the raids made a change in our uneventful lives and we quite enjoyed them."

Later that month Maria Boucher and her sister, whose company had been such a help to Monica, were transferred with some two hundred French women prisoners to the Ravensbrück concentration camp near Stettin in North Germany. There seemed to be no hard-and-fast rules as to who among women prisoners was to be sent to a penitentiary like Cottbus and who would end up in concentration camps. The decision was up to the camp's commandant. In this case it was obvious that the formidable *Direktorin* Gertrude Sauchel was out to take revenge on her French-speaking charges. Maria Boucher survived Ravensbrück. After the war she returned to her hometown, Liège, and wrote a moving letter to Monica's daughter, recalling "notre chère Monica's amazing fortitude of spirit, which influenced us all during our days together in cell 12."

* * *

As the days shortened and the long winter set in and bitter cold permeated the cells, Monica's strength began to ebb away. The long stint in West Prison, where each day she had expected to be led out to be executed, and nearly six months in Cottbus were beginning to take their toll on a woman unaccustomed to hardship. Her indomitable spirit was unbroken, but physically she was now a shadow of herself. Only the huge, extraordinary eyes remained and the beautiful emaciated hands, reminiscent of Dürer's painting. Only one letter from home had so far reached her (mail was disrupted by the saturation bombing), a brief postcard on a Red Cross letter form. Finally, in early December, two more letters arrived and two welcome parcels with cigarettes, a few clothes, toiletries, and the most desired article of all, real soap. She decided to start preparations for a Danish Christmas in prison.

There were now five Danish women in cell 12. Tulle Fiil of the Hvidsten group arrived in November, having been held in solitary confinement in Rostock for three months. She was soon joined by another Danish girl, Alice Bergman-Jensen, from the same Resistance unit in Jutland. Both women had been in Denmark during the uprising in the capital in June. "Your name was mentioned all through that historic week," Tulle told Monica. "Sentencing you to death provoked such nationwide fury against the Germans that it became the first step in the events leading to the mass Copenhagen uprising. Since then all executions have been stopped."

Unlike Monica, the young girls suffered more acutely from hunger than from cold and constantly fantasized about food. "I don't believe that one can ever imagine how much one thinks about food if one is forever hungry," recalled Pia. "Tulle and I kept listing the delicious things we would eat when we finally got home. We agreed that after we had been with the family for a while, we would go down to Mrs. Wich-feld's estate near Maribo, where we would each lie on a soft, clean bed and be served one delicious course after an-other. . . . In the meantime, we had to be content with slices of rye bread, which contained much more sawdust than rye, a thin soup, and occasionally a few potatoes which we ate hungrily, skin and all. . . . I don't want to advertise Macleans toothpaste, but it tastes quite good spread on bread, if you are hungry enough."

A week before Christmas the girls were sent to work in the local gas-mask factory on a 7 a.m. to 7 p.m. shift. Monica stayed behind. She busied herself cleaning the cell and mak-ing it as homelike as possible for Christmas, a tough assign-ment. She managed to make a tablecloth out of white paper napkins from her home parcels and cut out small, beautiful red paper roses. Using the Indian corn leaves with which they had been supplied for mat-making, she had made presents for her companions. Tulle got slippers, Pia a lovely little bas-ket, others got necklaces. A fir branch picked on a walk in the courtyard and carefully hidden under the bed became a Christmas tree, decorated with paper cutouts. The slices of bread which they had been saving for that evening were each decorated with bits of cheese. The tiny bits of silver paper found in food parcels became silver stars. When the girls got back from the factory, their Christmas table was ready. Here is Tulle Fiil's account of that Christmas, written in December 1945, after the war:

"Five Danish women: Mrs. Wichfeld, Pia, Grete, Alice, and I are spending Christmas in our little home—cell no. 12 at Cottbus. We have a real 'Christmas table' arranged by Mrs. Wichfeld and we decided that tonight we are not going to go to bed hungry. We each have four slices of bread, an onion,

2 1 8) M O N I C A

a carrot, a beet, and a small piece of red cabbage and two potatoes. Our Danish *smörgåsbord* is ready. To our eyes it looks delicious. Now we are waiting for our dinner, for they [the wardens] surely are bound to give us something extra. The door opens. We stand ready with our bowls, but how disappointed we are—only a piece of bread and ersatz coffee. But yes, there is also a slice of cheese. However, we shall not allow this to lower our spirits—after all we have our lovely *smörgåsbord*. We sit down at the table and eat and refuse to think of the roast goose at home. . . . We then take each other by the hand and Mrs. Wichfeld begins to sing 'Glade Jul.' How beautiful it sounds, but we only manage to finish the first verse. It's difficult to sing when you have a lump in your throat. . . . As usual Mrs. Wichfeld saves the evening and raises our spirits by beginning to distribute her presents: small, exquisitely wrapped parcels. . . . She has even been able to organize a few cigarettes. They will be much enjoyed when we get to bed. . . . Now the light is turned off at the mains by the wardens and we grope around in the dark, saying good night to each other and thanking each other for this evening. . . . Silence falls. It is almost midnight. But no . . . suddenly we hear a swelling chorus, Christmas carols being sung in other cells in every language—French, Dutch, Norwegian, Russian, Polish, German. . . . We lie quietly and listen. It's fortunate that the lights are out and that no one can see us and know what we feel."

We can only imagine what Monica's thoughts may have been that night. She well knew that her life was ebbing away. Only a few stitches remained in the tapestry of her life.

By the end of January rumors were circulating that the Russians were poised just outside Cottbus, for the prisoners could hear the heavy guns firing. In fact, the front was still about fifty miles east of Cottbus and was to remain there for some time. At this point the Germans decided to evacuate their foreign prisoners west to Waldheim, a small hill town between Dresden and Leipzig.

Ten

The Moonbeam

"OUR DESCENT INTO HELL" was how Monica's companions described the journey from Cottbus to Waldheim. It took three days and three nights for the cattle train to cover this short distance. Awakened at daybreak, the women were made to march to the station in deep snow, clad only in their flimsy prison garb. All 180 of them were crammed into three cattle cars, while the wardresses with their mountains of luggage occupied the three regular compartments next door. There was neither straw nor hay in the cars, only the filthy bare boards and the inevitable *Kübel*, soon spilling over from the motion of the train. Though the doors were sealed and outside temperatures hovered below freezing, the cold inside was intense. No food was dispensed on the journey, but in the foetid conditions it was not hunger that plagued the prisoners but thirst. A single bowl of water was passed around on the first day, barely enough for six.

When demands and cries rose for more water, Hilda, the wardress from Cottbus, seized a large water flask, held it aloft for a moment, then deliberately poured its precious contents

over the heads of the nearest women. It was an act of hatred
and of the purest, concentrated evil. Hilda shrugged her
shoulders and walked back to rejoin the others in the comfort
of their compartment.

Emil Viereck, pastor of the Lutheran church at Waldheim, was surprised when ordered by the town's military commandant to prepare his church as a reception center for the
arrivals from Cottbus. Waldheim was overflowing with refugees fleeing west before the advancing Russian armies. He
was told that there was no other place to put the 180 women
prisoners. A compassionate and humane man, Viereck worried that there was almost nothing he could do to ease their
plight. No medical supplies, food, or warm clothes were available in the neighborhood, or for that matter anywhere
else in the crumbling Reich. He decided to go to the station,
meet the transport, and see what he could do. The station was
crowded with soldiers. "It was icy cold," he recalled, "yet the
women who emerged from the cattle train were forbidden to
wrap blankets around themselves, lest it give the impression
of sloppy discipline. I found the sight of helpless females being
herded down the road by armed soldiers horrifying. Most of
them could barely drag one foot after another and stumbled
over the ruts in the road."

His attention was drawn to one woman, whose proud
bearing set her apart from the rest of the crowd. She held her
head high. "You will never get me down, no matter what you
do," she seemed to be saying to her captors. "That was how
I first saw Monica Wichfeld. The next time I found myself in
her presence, she was dying." The march from station to
church was Monica's final effort; the nightmare train journey
from Cottbus destroyed the last shred of her physical resistance. She collapsed when brought into Viereck's church, un-

able to swallow even a mouthful of the soup that was being distributed. Orders had gone out that the Cottbus prisoners for once were to be allowed to eat their fill, as they had been deprived of food for so long. "It was only a noodle soup they gave us, but Tulle and I had about five pints each—we were so starved," Pia wrote in her reminiscences. Room was made for Monica to lie down on one of the wooden pews in the church; she was burning with fever and racked with a cough. Despite this, she was for a time put in a cell with a woman dying of TB. After a week she developed viral pneumonia, but because typhoid was suspected and the wardresses were afraid it might spread, they allowed her to be transported to the sick ward.

As Monica's ordeal at Waldheim was nearing its final, tragic denouement, a figure stepped onstage amid the smoldering ruins of the war. Count Folke Bernadotte, the distinguished humanitarian and soldier, nephew of Gustav V, vice chairman of the Swedish Red Cross, opened up secret negotiations to bring about a speedy end to the war and arrange the release of all Danish and Norwegian prisoners.

"Isn't it pointless to continue the struggle?" Bernadotte asked Himmler on February 19 in Berlin. The Allies, having liberated France, Belgium, and the Netherlands, were poised to cross the Rhine, while the Russians were within a day's drive of Berlin. Desperate though their situation was and conscious that Armageddon was near, Himmler decided that Bernadotte's proposal was premature. He could not yet face the consequences of the inevitable final collapse. In conversation that day, the Reichsführer gave Bernadotte his answer: "Every German will fight like a lion before he ever gives up. You may think it sentimental, even absurd, but I have sworn loyalty to

Adolf Hitler, and as a soldier and a German I cannot deny my oath. I owe all I am to Hitler. How can I now betray him? I have built the SS on the basis of loyalty to each other. How can I abandon them?"*

Bernadotte did manage to obtain Himmler's permission to move all Danish and Norwegian prisoners into one camp at Malmö, Sweden, where they would remain until the end of the war under the care and protection of the Swedish Red Cross. The arrangements took some time, and Bernadotte, at great personal peril, had to return to Berlin a number of times to argue with Himmler's assistants (he twice escaped being buried under the wreckage of a bombed-out building). Late in March a fleet of blue-and-white Swedish buses, complete with highly trained medical personnel and stocks of food, crossed over from Malmö into Germany, bringing joy and liberation to imprisoned Scandinavian nationals.

"On April 10 we were fetched from our cells at Waldheim by the wardresses, who had suddenly become extraordinarily friendly," wrote Pia. "We came down to find a large handsome white-and-blue bus with a Danish flag painted on it. The driver smiled at us and called in Danish, 'Welcome, girls!' Tulle and I fell on each other's necks, overflowing with happiness." Thus thousands of people were rescued. In May, after the end of the war, Bernadotte set off to help other concentration-camp victims. More than 20,000 inmates of Hitler's camps owed their life to Count Folke Bernadotte and to the Swedish Red Cross.

Sadly, Monica was not among them. Would she have

---

*Two months later, on April 24, Himmler sought out Bernadotte and asked him to transmit a peace offer to the Allies that Germany surrender unconditionally to the United States and Great Britain, but not to the Soviet Union. The offer was rejected.

fought for her life had she known that deliverance was near? Would it have given her the strength to survive the remaining six weeks until her rescue? It is impossible to know.

The evening of February 27 was still and frosty. A full moon, which Monica could see from her hospital bed, hung over Waldheim. All her life she had harbored a particular affinity for the moon; she watched its path through the sky and admired its cold, distant beauty. "I had had an affair with the moon, in which there was neither sin nor shame," she often quoted from Laurence Sterne's poem, to her children, who teased her about her "lunar infatuation." This had its origin in the days of her Irish childhood, when she and Jack used to walk on the cliffs of Donegal's coast by moonlight and climb a magical "staircase to the moon." That evening, when Pastor Viereck came into her room, Monica asked him to open the window wide so she could see the moon through the bars. He did so. When he returned to the bed, Monica lay serene on the pillow with a beam of moonlight crossing her face. She had stopped breathing.

Viggo was walking down Copenhagen's main street on an afternoon in late March, when a Danish Red Cross worker he knew came toward him. "You ought to be at Engestofte with your family," she said with compassion. "We have just transmitted very sad news." Pastor Viereck's letter, sent through the channels of the Danish Red Cross, told Jorgen Wichfeld of the circumstances of his wife's death. It also described her heroic behavior and how her bearing and courage left an unforgettable impression. "It will always remain a memory of something beautiful," he wrote. He relayed her final messages to her husband, family, and children. "To her husband she said her last thoughts were of him in gratitude for his loyalty and affection." Pastor Viereck described her burial in the churchyard and gave Jorgen the number of the grave. Monica, who had been an agnostic since her brother Jack's death, had evidently regained her faith, since it was at her request that the pastor came to see her. Thus the circle of her life was completed.

Afterward, when peace came and the Iron Curtain descended, Waldheim became part of the Russian zone of occupation; contact with Pastor Viereck could not be maintained. The churchyard was overrun by Soviet troops and the church itself was badly damaged. It was months before the Russians allowed into Waldheim a special Danish commission delegated to bring back Monica's remains for reburial in the family churchyard at Engestofte. But when the grave was dug up, it was empty. Her body has never been found.

Epilogue

ON MAY 4, 1945, four days after Hitler's suicide in Berlin, his successor, Admiral Dönitz, authorized the capitulation of all German forces in northwest Germany and in Denmark. With this order the German resistance collapsed. The news of the capitulation was broadcast to Denmark by the BBC, and on that evening the people took to the streets in jubilation. Blackout curtains were torn down, lighted candles appeared in the windows, church bells rang. The Danish flag, "Dannebrog," was hoisted on every house. The Resistance Army, now some 43,000 strong, stood ready to maintain peace and order. The Danish Brigade, which had been training in Sweden, crossed over the sound at Elsinore. King Christian, having appointed a new government under Vilhelm Bühl (composed of an equal number of politicians and Resistance leaders), drove in triumph with his queen from Amalienborg, where they had for so long been virtual prisoners of the Germans, to Christiansborg to open the first peacetime parliament. Later that week he received the victorious General Montgomery in his palace. On Monty's orders, the 200,000

German troops who had laid down their arms the week before marched out of Denmark, carrying only their personal belongings and hand weapons. At the frontier they were searched, disarmed, and made to surrender Danish money. The country was freed without having had to endure the effects of Germany's "scorched-earth" policy. The five-year-long occupation of Denmark had ended.

At that time Flemming and Varinka Muus were in London, where they had been ordered by SOE before Christmas, just as the Gestapo ring was closing around them. They crossed over to Sweden in separate boats by the underground route and were reunited in Stockholm. The RAF flew them to London, where Flemming Muus was received by George VI and decorated for valor. Everywhere they were fêted as heroes, but later that spring Varinka's happiness was marred by the news of her mother's death.

On April 12 a moving memorial service was held in the Church of St. Saviour in London for Monica de Wichfeld, "the heroine of the Danish underground." Besides the family and her many friends, it was attended by the Danish ambassador in London, Count Edward Reventlow, representatives of the British Foreign Office, the Strategic Operations Executive (SOE), and Danish Resistance leaders working in England. "This service is more than a family expression of grief," said the Reverend Dean John Seymour, a longtime friend of Alice Massy-Beresford. "Monica, whom we remember today, gave her life for two nations. When her adopted country came beneath the tyranny of the conqueror, she lived to inspire her countrymen to preserve their faith in the resurrection of their land. She died for it."

Flemming and Varinka Muus returned to Denmark after the war to join Jorgen and the rest of the family at Engestofte.

They then moved into a house of their own in the outskirts of Copenhagen, where Flemming Muus died in 1982 and where his wife continues to live.

Jorgen, embittered and sad, continued to live at Engestofte until his death in July 1966. The estate was now prospering, the result of wise administration by the trustees and the excellent prices paid for farm products all through the war. The debts had been paid up and Jorgen could live in great comfort. Ironically it all came too late for Monica to enjoy. Throughout her years in the beautiful house that she loved there had been only a few moments when she was free of financial worry. As her brother Tim Massy-Beresford recalled, Jorgen "rattled about the house in solitary state, employing a staff of servants, who soon became so precious in Denmark that he dared not invite people to stay in case they should give notice because of the extra work."

Ivan, the older son and heir, and his beautiful wife, Hanne, were divorced shortly after the war. He went off to America, where he married an American, Rhoda Cameron Clark. He became a bridge player of international standing, a talent inherited from his parents. At the age of forty, he died of cancer in the winter of 1957. After Jorgen Wichfeld's death, Engestofte reverted to Viggo, who had been living abroad and worked for Shell. He and his Scottish wife returned to Denmark in the late sixties, but eventually the house and the estate were sold. I visited it with Viggo in 1987; the lake is magically beautiful and the house still bears Monica's imprint. I also went to see Rosenlund, Kurt's former house, and the palatial estate of Hardenberg, where Heini Haugwitz-Reventlow lived in splendor. Heini spent the last year of the war in Sweden, as his house had been taken over by German military authorities; it was later filled with refugees from

Schleswig-Holstein. After the war he lived there until his death, when it passed to a distant nephew in England. It is now being run as a prosperous modern farm, full of young children's voices and laughter.

Kurt Haugwitz-Reventlow, after his divorce from Barbara Hutton, lived first in France, then in the United States. On July 30, 1942 (three weeks after Barbara married Cary Grant), Reventlow married Margaret (Peggy) Astor-Drayton; they had one son. He continued to keep in touch with Viggo and with Monica's brother Tim, who was Lance Reventlow's (Barbara and Kurt's son) trustee. He would never return to Engestofte but visited Viggo in Rome. Kurt could never mention Monica's name without showing visible emotion; his wife, Peggy, said to Viggo: "I owe all that is nicest in my husband to your mother." In August 1969 Viggo heard that Kurt had died in New York after an operation.

Alice Massy-Beresford returned to her beloved Rapallo as soon as the war ended. She found Campo dei Fiori untouched, just as she had left it; the servants had looked after it with touching devotion. But the effects of the war, Monica's death, and her son's imprisonment in a Japanese camp (Brigadier Massy-Beresford returned to England after the Japanese surrender and pursued his distinguished military career) had undermined her fragile constitution. She made one more trip to London to introduce Ivan's wife, Rhoda, to her side of the family. She then telegraphed Olga Signorini at Rapallo: "Meet me in Milan—I am coming home to die." Indeed, she did die shortly thereafter.

The memory of Monica lives on in Denmark, although several generations have grown up since the war and details of the occupation have gradually faded. There was a time, however, when every Danish man, woman, and child knew of her. "You have become a legend in your lifetime," said a letter from a Jutland fisherman, which was smuggled to her at the West Prison. Since Denmark is a small country, many people knew of Monica and the Wichfeld family before the war, but her Resistance work, the dramatic circumstances of her arrest, and her amazing courage in prison, where she refused to give away the names of her collaborators, caught the nation's imagination. By the time of her trial in May 1944 she had become identified with Denmark's ardent newborn patriotism. She inspired many others to resist, while within the Resistance movement itself she not only symbolized purity of motive but served as a model for those who fell into enemy hands.

Her death had a profound effect; she was widely mourned by the public as well as by her family and friends. In a spontaneous gesture the staff and the people in and around Engestofte collected funds and installed a tablet in the local church. Since King Christian by then was too ill to take part in the ceremony, the queen unveiled it. In the ancient church of Derrylin in Northern Ireland, on the shores of Lough Erne, where she grew up, Monica's name has been added to the Roll of Honour of those who gave their lives in World War II. Monica's destiny unfolded between Lough Erne and the lake in faraway Scandinavia, the two lands she loved, and for which she gave her life.

Acknowledgments

IT WAS VIGGO, Monica's son, who had always been close to his mother, who first suggested I write her biography. He provided me with personal documents and letters, family reminiscences and photographs; without him, there would have been no book. Monica's brother Brigadier Massy-Beresford talked to me about their childhood in Ireland and contributed valuable insights into the characters of the various members of the family. I also wish to thank Monica's daughter, Mrs. Varinka Wichfeld-Muus, herself a heroine of the Danish Resistance, for her cooperation and help.

Many people in Denmark have been of assistance, and I would like to express my particular thanks to Mr. Svend Truelsen, and to the Librarian of the Museum of the Danish Resistance in Copenhagen, the Rigsarkivet and the Bundesarchiv in Coblenz. Baron and Baroness Bertouch-Lehn, their son Eric, and his wife Camilla were wonderfully hospitable during my visit to Denmark and enabled me to appreciate the beauty of Copenhagen and the Lolland countryside. I also wish to thank Miss Estelle Holt for combing the relevant war material and Foreign Office dispatches from Stockholm in the Public Records Office at Kew, and Miss Mary Young for her unfailing interest and good humor in typing yet another book for me. I am fortunate to have had the editorial guidance of Mr. Robert Giroux of Farrar, Straus and Giroux in New York.

London
November 12, 1989

Index